How to Find Your First Job Out of College

or
"Isn't There a Graduate Course on This?"

Sarah Hart

BURNING GATE PRESS
LOS ANGELES

For information address:
Burning Gate Press
P. O. Box 6015
Mission Hills, California 91395-1015

FIRST EDITION

Library of Congress Catalog Card Number 91-73713

ISBN 1-878179-05-5

Acknowledgments

I would like to thank the following employers for sharing their insights about job hunting with me: Colette Abissi, IBM; Peter Bowen, General Electric; Terri Goslin-Jones, Perpetual Bank; John Stewart, The Austin Company; John Stone, Chrysler; James Sturtz, General Motors, and Darrell Washington, Ford Motor Company.

I would also like to thank career counselors Sherrie Pavol Bereda, Career Concepts; Marilyn Goldman, Horizons Unlimited Inc.; Dr. Ray Harrison, Manchester, and Susan Schubert, Schubert & Associates, as well as psychologists Dr. Anita Auerbach and Dr. Diane Goebes.

Special thanks to Paul Ochs, Publisher of DataTrends Publications Inc., for providing me with the opportunity to go out on my own as a full-time free-lance writer and therefore have the time to write this book.

Contents

How to Find Your First Job Out of College

or

"Isn't There a
Graduate Course on This?"

GETTING OFF TO A GRAND START...
If Only I Had A Syllabus For The Rest Of My Life

"Our grand business in life is not to see what lies
dimly at a distance but to do what clearly lies at hand."
—Thomas Carlyle

Graduating from college is an exciting experience. It opens
the door to a new stage in your life and gives you an opportunity to explore the unexpected. Along with the chance to make
some new discoveries, however, graduation from college can
also bring confusion and anxiety as you struggle to decide
exactly what you're going to do with the rest of your life.

If you're torn by conflicting emotions, exhilarated about
embarking on another phase of life but terrified by the idea of
looking for a job, you're probably like most other college
seniors or recent graduates. Luckily, you can turn your
nervousness into energetic optimism simply by plunging into
your job hunt.

And you've taken the first step by starting to read this book. Using this book, you can gain an understanding of what employers are looking for in a job applicant. You can draw on the advice and opinions of recruiters from some of America's largest companies, and you can use it to figure out what makes or breaks an interview...or a resume...or a cover letter. And since this advice is written from the point of view of someone who was recently in your shoes, you can feel confident that it truly applies to you.

If you're the way I was when I graduated, you probably have one particular job hunting question that overshadows everything else you do. It may seem silly in retrospect, but my job hunting question caused me endless trauma. From an objective point of view, the issue which I was pondering was insignificant. From my perspective, however, it was monumental. Does this sound familiar?

My problem was that I didn't know what to wear to an interview. As the months leading to graduation sped by, my world view narrowed. I went from thinking about the state of the world to worrying about my future to obsessing about my interview clothes. Fortunately, this embarrassing transformation wasn't visible to my outwardly confident friends.

In fact, I realized later that they too were worrying about one aspect or another of the challenges and of the job hunt that lay before them. The truth is that almost all college seniors have some job worry that plagues them through those final glorious days of school.

Fortunately, I managed to get over my misplaced anxiety over interview clothes, and I eventually found something appropriate to wear. But I know how it feels to search for answers to your most basic job hunting questions, secretly doubting the conflicting advice you get from everyone you speak to.

Whether your job hunting questions regard interview clothing or networking, resume writing techniques or decision making strategies, this book can help you feel more confident about your decisions.

The Benefits Of Job Hunting

As you begin your job hunt, think about what you're going to be gaining over the next few weeks or months. Job hunting can yield future contacts, valuable references, interesting part-time jobs and internships and a wealth of new experiences.

O.K., so you're willing to skip all that if you can just find a great job tomorrow. While most of us feel that way, job hunting can actually be an enriching experience. Unfortunately, most people our age see job hunting only as something you do to find a job and not as something that has any merit in itself. However, job hunting can be part of a greater scheme of uncovering not only what type of job you want but what type of person you are. According to one of the head college recruiters at Ford Motor Co., as you look for a job, you can figure out how you want to spend your life

This comes from understanding more about the companies you interview with and from understanding more about the working world in general.

"In understanding an organization, we can relate it to our own experience and develop a career plan," says Darrell Washington, college recruiting and central placement manager at Ford Motor Company in Dearborn, Michigan.

"So much of one's success in the future depends upon one's ability to fit into an organization, not just the ability to put together the cognitive pieces," notes Washington.

By looking for a job, you can make informed decisions based upon a good understanding of what kind of job you want and where that job is. The most important part of your job search is you—your attitude, your interests, your life-style and your approach to job hunting. Getting started on the right foot can make or break your job search, as well as your spirit and your budget. And sometimes getting started is the hardest part.

Doing What Lies At Hand

According to Dr. Anita Auerbach, a psychologist in McLean, Virginia, many recent graduates experience a paralysis born both of perfectionism and a fear of failure. This kind of feeling can prevent you from beginning to look for a job and result in procrastination. And since most of us develop procrastination into a fine art while we're in college, we've had a little too much practice at putting things off.

"The temptation for college students is to say 'oh, I'll take the summer off,'" says Dr. Auerbach. "Then they lose their momentum and sometimes get into an inertia which carries them along."

One way to get out of this inertia, or avoid falling into it, is to split job hunting down into a series of manageable steps. This gives you a way to get started and a way to keep from feeling overwhelmed, according to another psychologist who helps a lot of job seekers.

"It helps to break [job hunting] down into very small steps. Say to yourself, this week, I'll make a list of companies, next week, I'll get the names of those in personnel, and the next week, I'll do a resume," suggests Dr. Diane Goebes, a Falls Church, Virginia-based psychologist experienced in career assessments.

"If you say, this week, I'll get a job, its overwhelming," adds Goebes.

In this chapter, we'll look at some preliminary steps you

can take to get geared up for job hunting. If you're already geared up, great. If not, you can be soon, if you'll establish a home office, decide how to support yourself while you're looking for a job and develop a daily schedule.

"I Still Get To Buy School Supplies?"

Setting up your home office is an excellent way to start your job hunt. While you may not be able to socialize in the office supply store quite like you could in your college bookstore, you might find buying office supplies to be a close substitute for your annual fall buying and browsing frenzy. Just don't ask the salesperson where the snacks, beer, posters and erasable memo boards are located.

Setting up a home office is helpful for both practical reasons and psychological reasons. First, it can help you get organized. When you start sending out resumes and making phone calls, you'll get a lot of mail in return. Much of this mail will be rejection letters, but that doesn't matter. You'll need to keep a copy of all the letters you send and all the letters you receive.

If you send a letter to Ms. Jones at Company X in May, get a rejection in June and then get called back in August, it's doubtful you'll even remember sending in the initial letter.

Since you'll be sending out a lot of letters to a lot of different employers for related but different jobs, you may not say exactly the same thing in each letter. Therefore, you'll need a well-organized home office so you can easily refer to your files to find what you said about yourself, your career goals and the job.

It's important to be consistent in what you say to each employer. This is fairly easy when you have a well organized filing system, but if you send out letters haphazardly and don't keep records of what you've done, you will be totally lost when someone calls you about a letter you sent them months ago.

When you're in college, it seems like everything starts over each semester. In April, no one really cares what you did in November. You probably don't even remember what you did in November.

When you're job hunting, things from the past have an unfortunate tendency to crop up a few months later, and it's somewhat embarrassing to be completely unaware of letters you've written.

If you have an office, you can keep files on letters sent out, letters that are still pending (you haven't heard from them, but it hasn't been that long), letters requiring some action or follow-up on your part, and outright rejections. We'll get into this in more detail later on.

Of Course I Work, I'm Job Hunting

Second, there are psychological reasons for setting up a home office. If you have an office, you'll see job hunting as a bona fide activity. Your home office will remind you that job hunting requires time and commitment.

A well-organized home office will also give you a way to measure how you're doing. You can feel a sense of accomplishment when you look over your files and realize all the things you've done in a given time frame.

You may be feeling a little skeptical right now, remembering how your mother told you you'd feel such a sense of accomplishment when you learned to play the piano. What an experience that turned out to be!

However, as you look for a job, you'll see how important it is to keep track of your small successes along the way. For example, if in one month of job hunting, you have three interviews, attend a job hunting seminar and meet a significant person in your desired line of work, you will have accomplished a lot.

This may not sound very meaningful if you aren't employed yet, but setting up a home office and charting your progress can keep you from getting discouraged. (If you're already discouraged, you might want to read Chapter 8, which covers burn out.)

If you live with eighteen of your closest friends and rarely spend time alone even in the bathroom, developing a home office may sound difficult. However, all it takes are some office supplies, a telephone, an answering machine, and a typewriter, or, if possible, a computer.

Home Office Basics

Here is a list of supplies you should consider buying:
Correction fluid
Notebook and typing paper
Files
Labels and envelopes
A stapler
Paperclips
Tape
Post-it notes
A scale to weigh mail
$25 worth of stamps

Larger investments might include a typewriter, an answering machine and a computer. Unless you already have a computer you used in college, it's probably not the first thing you want to buy when you graduate.

If possible, find a friend who has one at home. You might also see if one of your friends can let you go to their office after work hours to use their work computer. By now, that on-campus word processing center you used to hate is looking pretty attractive.

However, if you look hard enough, you can find a good and relatively inexpensive replacement for many of those campus amenities. Well, O.K., it's hard to replace that oh-so-versatile college I.D. that doubles as a credit card and door key and basically gets you in anywhere you want to go, but maybe having your own home office can make up for this loss.

If you don't have any friends who have access to their work computers after hours (or if you don't have any friends who are employed yet), most cities have professional printing and photocopying stores where you can use their computers by the hour. Look in the yellow pages under "printing," "typesetting," or "desktop publishing."

Sending out large mailings to hundreds of companies is greatly simplified when you have a computer. With a computer, you can make very small changes in one basic form letter which is cleverly written so it doesn't look like a form letter.

An answering machine is another great tool. With a machine, you won't miss important calls. And since you're going to be away from your phone interviewing, developing contacts, and yes, occasionally doing something fun, it's a good investment.

Besides, who knows what kinds of social opportunities you might have in this new life of yours? That answering machine could provide you with more than just an amazing job.

One career counselor suggests having two addresses and phone numbers printed on your resume if you've recently moved or if you have a lot of roommates and are difficult to reach.

You could consider putting your parents' number on your resume if you live in the same city or you could use the number of a reliable friend with an answering machine.

Job Hunting On A Budget

The biggest bind most people find themselves in after graduating is supporting themselves. It's funny how being jobless can make that difficult.

There are several options for job hunters. The best is to find some kind of part-time job or internship in your field.

This might mean working in a local university press office if you're interested in a public relations job, working part-time for a political candidate or state or national politician if you want a job related to political science, or working for an accounting firm if you're interested in a career in accounting.

Part-time jobs are not just a way to support yourself and to kill time. They can provide you with marketable experience and add to your list of future references.

Through a good part-time job, you might find yourself interested in some aspect of your chosen career field which you didn't know much about. This could lead you to pursue new options in that area. Part-time jobs are also valuable in that they can lead to full-time jobs.

If you can't find a paying part-time job, you may have to volunteer your time and work for free. If you need a job for income, this obviously isn't an option. However, if you can swing it, volunteer work can strengthen your resume as much as a paying part-time job. It could even lead to a paying full-time job.

Some professional career counselors believe your resume can benefit from volunteer work.

"If you can't find a paid job," says Susan Schubert, president of Schubert & Associates, a career development company in Columbus, Ohio, "volunteer to work an internship. This gives you references and solid work experience."

Volunteer work also gives you a lot of flexibility in setting up interviews.

For example, I had an unpaid internship one summer. Every time I would come in, my boss would jokingly check to make sure I wasn't late. He would usually pretend I was, and he would say, "I'm going to have to take this out of your paycheck."

While I didn't think this was as hilarious as he found it to be, it illustrates that you're pretty much your own agent in an unpaid position. You can get good work experience, make new contacts and schedule interviews at times that are best for you without having to worry about being penalized.

Volunteering your time is especially useful if you are interested in a field in which you don't have any formal training. You often have an opportunity to learn new skills, or to put classroom theory into practice.

Other options for part-time work include clerical work, such as "temping," retail jobs, or waiting tables. These kinds of jobs may be your best alternative if money is a problem, and you can't afford to work for free or to spend time looking for a paying part-time job in your field.

And, contrary to what you may think, working in a non-professional job while looking for a professional job does not weaken your resume.

Many employers are impressed by the discipline and motivation it takes to stick with more menial work while you're in college or shortly after you've graduated.

"I admire any work experience," says Terri Goslin-Jones, director of employment at Perpetual Savings Bank in Alexandria, Virginia. "We encourage part-time work while a student is in college, whether it's being a waiter or waitress or working in retail sales."

According to Goslin-Jones, banking is a very customer service-oriented field, and retail experience is valuable and relevant.

"Employers look highly on temp work," adds Sherrie Pavol Bereda, an account specialist with Career Concepts, Inc. in Macon, Georgia. "It shows some kind of ambition and drive."

Flexibility is another reason you might want to consider retail or restaurant jobs if you must work full-time. You can then work a half day and evening shift, giving yourself four or five good hours to devote to finding the job you really want.

Phone sales might be another option. In these positions, you often work evening hours so you can reach people while they're at home.

If you can, try to find a part-time job with shifts which would give you a few full days off on a regular basis. For example, you could work full-time for a few days and then have a few days off.

Methods for finding paid and volunteer part-time jobs will be discussed in the chapters on finding potential employers and networking.

The Fine Art Of Scheduling

Once you've set up your office and figured out how you're going to support yourself, you're ready to establish a schedule.

Setting up a schedule for yourself ties in with your attitude toward job hunting. If you act as though looking for a job is a real job, you will get a lot more done.

"Realize that looking for a job is a job in itself," urges Dr. Goebes. "If you decide to devote six hours a day to looking for a job, those are sacred hours. Don't go wax the floor."

This might mean looking at the day as a real 9 to 5 work experience. Get started with your calls or your letter writing or whatever goal you've set for yourself that day at 9:00 a.m. Take a normal lunch break and plug away for most of the afternoon.

If you aren't working at all while you're job hunting, you probably can give yourself a few free hours at some point just to have fun. But you'll be amazed at how busy you'll become as your job hunt expands.

Whether you need to spend eight hours a day job hunting or only four, it works best to regard job hunting as a legitimate activity requiring regular hours.

If you've just started your job hunt, it's hard to take a long-term view of it. While it can be depressing to approach it this way, it's not unusual for first time job seekers to look for weeks or months before finding the right job.

"It takes an average of six to eight months for recent college graduates to find a job," says Pavol Bereda.

I was astonished when I first heard that several years ago. When I graduated from college, I assumed it would only take me a few weeks to find a job. After all, I did have that interview suit.

Well, despite having found the perfect attire, it took me a few months. In the end, though, I found a challenging and fun job, after I turned down several things that wouldn't have been right for me (we'll discuss that more later in the chapter on choosing the right job).

I hesitate to set limits or say how long it will take you to find a job because it's such an individual process. It often comes down to being the person with the right credentials who happens to be in the right place at the right time.

Rather than try to guess at how long it will take you to find a job, it's best to establish an initial schedule, set short-term goals and get started.

In the beginning stages of your job hunt, you should devote half of the time you have available to job hunting. If you have four hours free, set aside two. If you have a full eight hour day, try to work on your job search for four.

Before I went to college, I did not take naps. After I graduated from college, I could hardly make it through the day without a nap. If you picked up this bad habit too, and your body is still on college time, you can schedule your job hunting around your nap time. I just wouldn't discuss this with any potential employers.

When you're beginning to look, setting aside more time will only frustrate and disappoint you. However, once you've gotten into your job hunt, you can establish your schedule so you're looking during most of your free hours. This isn't as grueling as it sounds, as looking can take many forms.

Meeting your friends for lunch is important, as you can keep up with what's going on at their offices and remind them you're still job hunting. It will also remind you that there are still people in the world who are your own age. It's such a change to go from a world populated by your eighteen to twenty-one year old peers who want to have a good time to a world populated by much older people who are actually serious about life.

Job hunting can make you feel like you're the youngest person on the face of the earth. Setting up your schedule so you see people your own age can help you keep your perspective.

As you can see, setting a schedule for yourself serves several different purposes, from insuring you're actually going to get something done each day to helping you maintain your enthusiasm for the job hunt.

You'll soon find that job hunting has a snowball effect. Once you start sending out resumes, networking and interviewing, the entire process builds upon itself. Eventually, you'll need more and more time to keep up with all of the things you're doing.

Your Game Plan For Reaching That Goal In The Distance

You'll want to vary the following step-by-step plan according to your own experience, time limits and individual circumstances.

1. Set up your home office within the next day or two. Stake out your space and decide where you will keep your files. You'll probably want your home office to be close to a phone because you'll eventually be making a lot of calls. It should only take a few hours for you to set up the basics. If you can afford it, buy all of the supplies you'll need now so you can have this behind you.

This is also the time to determine which library is the best one in your community for conducting a job search. Ask the reference librarian—some branches have special sections devoted to careers and job seeking and they are a good source of seminars on resumes, interviewing, etc. You should also make sure you have access to the newspaper(s) in the area in which you want to work, whether local or long distance. This way, you will have the classified ads close at hand, and you can easily read about the jobs that are available.

2. Work on your resume for the next week. Try to finish it completely within six or seven working days. Just to keep track of our timetable, you're now one week into your job hunt. To achieve this resume goal, read the resume chapter.

Decide how your resume can be improved. Have your friends look over it and make suggestions. If you think your resume is O.K. as it is, great. You've achieved your first goal!

This is another important concept in job hunting. If there is an area you've mastered, such as developing your resume or utilizing your contacts, skip over it and consider it a strong point. No one knows your job hunting situation better than you, and there may areas in which you don't need any help.

3. Develop your various cover letters within the next two weeks. (This puts you into week two or three of your job hunt). It helps to alternate between two tasks which both require concentration. When you feel burned out from working on your resume, work on your cover letter. The two go hand in hand, and you might get ideas for your resume when you're thinking about how you're trying to present yourself in your cover letter.

4. Within the next three weeks, find some places to send this excellent resume and cover letter you've developed. For ideas, read the chapter on finding employers. (If you're still counting, you're now three to four weeks into your job hunt.)

5. One week after you've sent out your resume and a cover letter to a list of employers, it's time to start your follow-up. You should be roughly into the first four or five weeks of your job hunt. Follow-up can be the most exciting, and for many recent graduates, the most intimidating part of the job hunting process.

Don't worry, though. Once you've studied the ten most common interview questions (found in this book in the chapter about interviewing) and you've practiced your responses to interview questions, you'll feel more confident about contacting potential employers to request an interview. It all comes down to preparation, and if you know what to expect when you place a follow-up phone call, you'll be able to make a positive first impression.

You'll want to hone and refine your interview style not just for the follow-up phone call that gets you in the door, but also for the interview itself. During the week that you place your follow-up phone calls (roughly week four of your job hunt), prepare for any interviews that might come up. Practice aloud with a friend, think through each sample interview question presented in this book and assemble your interview clothes.

6. As you carry out these specific parts of the job search, you'll want to utilize the rest of your time to engage in networking. Networking is a critical part of your job search, and it is something you should do throughout each stage of your hunt.

Therefore, when you start your networking overtures, you could be in week one of your job search, or you may be in week five. Ideally, the sooner you start networking, the better, but as we've discussed in the section about scheduling, you don't want to bite off more than you can chew at any one time.

When you decide the time is right for you, read the chapter on networking and figure out who you know...or who your friends know...or who you need to know to conduct an effective, successful job search. Networking enables you to make that person-to-person contact so essential in a job hunt, and it is a big part of coming to understand what it is that makes you happy in a job.

To get started on your networking journey, make a list of ten people to contact for an informational interview or a brief meeting. After you've established your job hunting routine, give these people a call.

7. After you've had a few interviews, start preparing for that decision-making process. Read the chapter on making decisions. This will give you information on how to judge a job on its merits and how to determine from the glowing interview description what it is you'd really be doing in that position.

While choosing a job sounds like the easy part of the job search, it can actually be the most wrenching. However, if you've given some thought to the specific responsibilities and overall office atmosphere you're seeking, you can make wise decisions with a minimum of difficulty.

As you're probably beginning to see, job hunting is as much a continual process as it is a series of discrete steps. The basic cycle of the job hunt consists of : 1) finding employers/ responding to want ads; 2) sending resumes and cover letters to the job or networking prospects you've found; 3) following up on those mailings in order to obtain an interview or to develop a new networking contact; 4) interviewing and following up with a thank you note; and 5) fielding job offers and selecting the job that is right for you.

It may sound a little overwhelming right now, but if you'll get started, you can establish a job hunting routine that will carry you through each step of the job search. The best news is that in reading this chapter and by giving some thought to your own step-by-step plan, you've already started your job search!

You're now one step closer to that goal that lies dimly at a distance, and you have some idea of what to expect in the days and weeks that lie ahead.

MAKING YOUR RESUME AN UNCOMMON SUCCESS...

Resume? I Thought All I Had To Do Was Sign Up Somewhere

"The secret to success is to do the common things uncommonly well."
—John D. Rockefeller, Jr.

Your resume is an important component of a successful job hunt. If you'll follow the tips outlined in this chapter, you can create a memorable resume reflecting your skills and interests to your best advantage.

A good resume is like a good ad. It catches the attention of potential employers, sparks their interest and lures them into the subject matter—you. A good resume is straight and simple. It reflects what you've done and shows your ability to build upon these experiences to prosper in the job market.

Career counselors stress the importance of keeping your resume brief and to the point.

"Employers aren't looking for a detailed life description," says career counselor Sherrie Pavol Bereda of Career Concepts. "They want to see something really organized, with education and work experience at the top."

Let's discuss each part of the resume and how it contributes to the whole. As a recent graduate, your resume should include:
   -your name, address and phone
   -your objective
   -your educational background and GPA
   -your work history
   -a few relevant social or community activities
   -your honors, awards or special achievements
   -membership in any professional groups
   -some mention of references

Your Name, Address and Phone

Hopefully, this part is not difficult for you. It's a good idea to include two addresses and phone numbers. One could be a permanent address, like your parents' address. This is good if you're still apartment hunting.

Your Objective

Some employers and career counselors recommend you include an objective; others don't. A good rule of thumb is to use an objective when you're applying for a job with a large corporation or a highly structured company.

Employers like this hire hundreds of people a year in many

different fields. They like to see an objective stated because it tells them of the type of job for which you're applying.

According to a top recruiter at Ford, the use of an objective gives an employer a better idea of your career plans and interests.

"We have opportunities in almost any area you can imagine," says Ford's Darrell Washington. "If students don't give an objective as to what they want to do with their education and work history, we end up playing a guessing game as to where they fit in."

If you're looking at a smaller or more specialized company which only hires a certain type of employee, you probably don't need an objective.

If you do use an objective, it should clearly describe the type of job for which you're looking. It should mention both the kind of work you want to do and the specific skills which enable you to do this job better than other applicants.

A good objective is narrow, employers say, and it pinpoints a particular job title.

"The objective should define the area of interest specifically," says John M. Stewart, corporate vice president of The Austin Company, a mid-sized engineering firm in Cleveland Heights, Ohio. "It shouldn't be a broad statement that says "I want to be in management.""

Remember that companies want to know what you can do for them rather than what they can do for you. Structure your resume and your objective to answer their question as to why they should hire you.

The best way to answer this question, according to career counselors, is to be direct. Don't get into a lot of lofty statements in your objective about your search for personal fulfillment.

"You look at a lot of objectives, and they say the person wants challenges and intellectual stimulation," says Dr. Ray

Harrison, executive vice president of Manchester, a career consulting firm, in Philadelphia, Pennsylvania. "Frankly, the employer could care less. The whole resume should be oriented towards what the employer wants."

"Don't use fancy overblown language," says career counselor Susan Schubert of Schubert & Associates. "I've seen resumes with objectives that read 'Seeking position with opportunity for personal growth with a high visibility role, etc.' Personnel people don't care about that."

Although you undoubtedly have skills which could be used in several similar jobs, your resume and your objective should target one specific job. Therefore, if you're going to use an objective, you'll need two or three different resumes, one for each objective.

Your Educational Background

Along with your work history, your educational background is the heart of your resume. It is crucial to depict your education as a tool which has prepared you well for your career. The more specific you are about the things you learned in school and how they will contribute to your future job performance, the better chance you'll have of obtaining an interview.

For example, in addition to listing the name of your college or university, the year you graduated, your GPA, your major and the type of degree you earned, you should include relevant course work.

I know, it hardly seemed relevant to your major, much less to a job. Nevertheless, career counselors believe you should use your academic experience as one of your strongest selling points.

"Most people try to match up their part-time or summer

jobs to the position they're seeking when they should be focusing more on content knowledge," Harrison adds, "such as a course they've taken."

For example, if you majored in computer science and you're looking for a job in information systems, list the computer science courses you took and include your GPA for your major. If you majored in political science and you're looking for a job with a state legislator, list the political science courses you took and include your GPA for those classes.

When highlighting your educational experience, you can also include courses you may have taken for fun during the summer. For example, if you took a class at a local community college, it could be an asset if it is related to the job you're seeking.

Your GPA And Any Academic Honors

Even if you did not do well in college, you should still include your GPA on your resume. Glossing over poor academic performance will only weaken your resume. When applicants don't list their GPA's, this immediately sounds warning bells for one employer.

Peter Bowen, a college recruiter at General Electric in Bridgeport, Conn., says, "When I see the resume of a recent college graduate and it doesn't have a GPA listed, that tells me it wasn't that great."

If your grades were low, you might stress that you carried a heavy load or a difficult mix of courses. If you worked during the school year and you had a lot of extra demands on your time, you might put that on your resume in some form.

You can make up for a lower GPA with hard-hitting work

experience, a double major or an unusual combination of courses (such as Calculus and English literature.)

It also helps if you can show that you made some sort of progress in your academic development. If your grades progressively improved over your college career, point that out. You can compensate for lower grades by stressing how successful you were in another area of college achievement or in your summer jobs.

Your Work History

Like academic performance, work history is a "must include" category. Unfortunately, while lifeguarding is fun, unless your boss happens to be drowning at some point, it may not be applicable to the job market.

"One thing that is obviously a problem for recent college graduates is that they don't have work experience or what they have isn't relevant," according to Harrison.

If that pretty much sums up your life to this point, don't despair.

If you did have some substantial jobs in which you used your major, or at least your brain, play them up. Emphasize all of the meaty things you did, even if you only had a chance to do each new task once and were closely supervised.

For example, if you worked for an ad agency and wrote a print and a radio ad, say what you did and how you did it. If you wrote these ads and they never ran, you can still mention you wrote them. Stress the skills you learned when you undertook this exercise.

You could say, "Wrote six print and broadcast media ads for retail clothing store client. Utilized graphics skills for print ads; learned to limit word usage and paint verbal picture for broadcast media ads."

If you worked for an ad agency, but you didn't get a chance to write any ads, tell about what you learned from observing others write ads. Say how you would put these principles into practice if you were to get the job for which you are applying.

For example, on your resume you could say, "Summer internship for advertising/public relations firm specializing in clients in the arts. Worked closely with account supervisor; attended client meetings; learned how to meet client demands on limited budget. As result of internship, familiar with copywriting process and approvals procedure."

Be as specific as possible, and be sure to take credit for developing an idea yourself, even if it was only reorganizing a company's filing system or developing a more efficient way for them to collect money for a mundane office expense, like a communal candy tray.

While your actual idea might be related to something trivial, it demonstrates that you took initiative to solve problems.

Improving Your Resume

One career counselor suggests focusing on results to give your resume increased impact.

"Start each paragraph with a verb—developed, initiated, created," says Marilyn Goldman, president of Washington, D.C.-based Horizons Unlimited Inc., a career consulting firm. "What were your accomplishments? If you had an internship or summer work or a research paper that got results, say so."

Discussing results often means giving specific examples of what you did, adds Schubert.

"You want a resume to document and support," comments Schubert. "This means giving examples of what you did at a summer job or how you gained a new skill."

Schubert believes a lot of recent college graduates have good experience but are too vague in the way they word their resumes.

"One error is that [applicants] talk about wonderful things without giving examples," Schubert adds.

To illustrate that your ideas were highly regarded at a summer job, mention something an employer changed at your urging. Perhaps you suggested to the personnel department that the summer internship application form be expanded to include a brief summary of the intern's goals for the summer. This way, you explained, interns could be certain of getting the most out of their internships and the company would be certain of getting the most out of their interns.

On your resume, you might say "Suggested changes to summer internship form which better informed Company XYZ of interns' goals. Company XYZ made changes and reported better intern and staff satisfaction with program."
If you didn't have any substantial job experience while you were in college, maybe you can transform something you did that was unusual into an attractive and interesting statement.

If you played a menial role in a glamourous field, and you are now seeking a job in that same field, play it up. I knew a guy who wanted to be a doctor. One summer, he worked as a messenger boy carrying lab samples around town. It sounded like a disgusting job, and he had these wild stories about dropping medical samples in the middle of intersections.

While he thought he didn't do anything of substance, and I never saw his resume, he could have used that job to his advantage when applying for medical school or when looking for an even better job the next summer.

For example, he could point out his familiarity with medical labs, his knowledge of the testing process and his ability to withstand the more gruesome side of the medical profession.

"Did I Mention I Filled In For The President Last Summer?"

However, the flip side of this is not to make something totally worthless sound bigger than it was.

First, it's dishonest. Second, seasoned human resources people will see through that immediately. Pretending that a low level job was something impressive makes the rest of your resume weaker.

You might be disqualifying yourself when you were otherwise a good candidate, both because employers are put off by false pretenses and because they wonder if anything on your resume is true.

For example, here are two different ways of describing a waitressing job. You can see how easy it is to tell when someone is basically filling up their resume with overly flattering descriptions.

1. "Served as primary waitress for large, fast-paced restaurant. Responsible for food service, decor, and customer satisfaction. Worked closely with manager. Closed out cash register at end of the night."

2. "Worked as culinary server for dining establishment catering to corporate clientele. Assisted maitre d'; advised manager in financial transactions."

If a job seeker were to word her resume like the second example, it would sound like she had worked as a waitress but wanted to appear she was a chef, a diplomat and the company's chief financial officer.

Play up your jobs and put in specifics—whether it was developing an internship program or building up some kind of reference tool — but don't overdo it. Just use your common sense.

Social and Community Activities

Another tricky area for recent college graduates is which social activities to include and what to say about them.

There is a fine line between showing you did occasionally get out of the library and having a resume that would get you a job organizing parties on a cruise ship (although as jobs go, that might not be a bad one).

In general, career counselors don't think you should include a lot of detail about your social life.

"A personal history, like hobbies or social activities, really isn't necessary," says Pavol Bereda.

So use restraint in including social activities. If you include them, mention only two or three. Try to make some reasonable correlation between the skills you used in these activities and the skills you will be using on the job.

For example, if you were the treasurer of a social organization and you're looking for a job in finance, you should list what you did and how you learned from this experience. You could say "I oversaw a $2000 budget, developed a new billing system and put the organization in the black for the first time in three years."

According to Pavol Bereda, if you do include a lot of social activities on your resume, you should delete them after you have been out of college for a few years.

Honors, Awards, and Special Achievements

This should probably be reworded as Honors, Awards and Things You've Done You Didn't Realize Were Special Achievements. Keeping in mind that you don't want to exaggerate and make a big deal out of activities that weren't that important, you can still find a way to promote yourself to employers.

If you won any awards, list them and mention what the competition was like. For example, you could say, "Recognized for achievement in Spanish Literature," or "First student in history of award to receive unanimous faculty vote" or "Won $1000 scholarship for further study of physics after scoring in top tenth percentile on departmental exam."

If you didn't receive any formal awards or honors, you still may have excelled in a particular area of college achievement.

This is the part of your resume where you can play up the things you did. It's easy to assume you don't have anything to put in an Honors and Awards category on a resume if you didn't get any formal awards, but if you think about it, there probably is something you can list.

If you were a big player in campus politics and won several elections, list that. Mention how it added to your organizational and leadership skills.

If you received personal recognition from a faculty member for your contribution to the department as a teaching assistant, you can put that in the Honors and Awards category.

It's often hard to see smaller bits of recognition as an honor or award, but the trick is to think of something you did in college where a professor or student organization praised you for your participation. As long as this informal "award" is genuine and reflects one of your strong points, you can list it in the awards section.

Obviously, you wouldn't want to include something trivial, like the time you received a form letter from some sort of charitable organization. However, if you organized a college fund-raiser for a charitable organization and got a personal letter of thanks from the regional vice president, that would qualify as Something You've Done You Didn't Realize Was A Special Achievement.

Just use your judgment in this category and look carefully over all of your college activities. College projects may not pose the same demands as those in the real world of careers, but they can take a tremendous amount of time, energy, effort and intelligence.

Of course, not all college projects are worthwhile for everyone who participates in them. I remember visiting a friend of mine at another college during my junior year and somehow becoming a part of his "class project."

For this project, his entire literature class was forced to act out scenes from an Ibsen play one cold October night in his professor's garage. I remember watching him and his class-mates gorge on the Oreo cookies and wine provided by their professor as they presented scenes from various plays they had read that semester.

I thought the whole evening was a strange experience, and for me, this project would not have been a high point of my college career. You've probably participated in some college projects that wouldn't be too helpful for your resume or your future job hunting efforts as well.

However, there are probably some things you did in college that took a lot of time and effort. Be proud of your collegiate accomplishments and play them up in a resume when you can.

Membership In Professional Associations

Most career fields have organizations in which practitio-ners of the job get together and discuss common concerns.

It's a great way to meet people in your field and to learn about new jobs, so if you didn't belong to any student chapters of professional associations while you were in college, this is a good time to join.

As far as your resume goes, if you did belong to any of these groups, be sure to list them. It shows you thought about career advancement while you were in college.

References Available

It's important to put across the bottom of your resume that several people will act as references for you. Most employers take references very seriously and will follow up with the names you give them.

You should try to have three or four references. Most employers ask for three. If you have four, you can give them three names and keep your other one on hold.

Alternate your references, so that the same people, whether they're professors or former employers, don't get swamped with calls about you. You should ask your references if they'll serve as references for you, and you should let them know each time they'll be receiving a call.

It's also a good idea when you ask people to serve as references to confirm they can say something positive about you. If for some reason a potential reference is not comfortable giving you a positive reference, it will be easier on both of you if you find that out now.

When you ask professors (or former employers) if they will serve as one of your references, simply say, "Do you feel there is something positive you could mention from my class performance (or my summer internship)? Would you be able to recommend me for the job if an employer calls you?"

It's most likely your professor or former employer will say

yes, especially if you perceived the relationship to be a positive one, but it never hurts you to be sure that your references will be providing you with a true recommendation. It will hurt your chances for getting a job if your reference indicates he or she was not fully pleased with your performance.

If your potential reference does not want to give you a positive recommendation, he or she will probably tell you that anyway. However, in asking if the comments will be positive, you can be absolutely certain.

Professors and former employers hold equal weight, and both will do fine as references. You can never have too many references, and this is a good time to solidify those ties with your professors. It's easier to establish ties with a professor now than it is three years after you've graduated. We'll get into this more in the chapter on networking.

The Perfect Format

Even though you've determined the content of your resume, you're still confronted with the question of how to lay it out on the page. Deciding how to format your resume can be a confusing process.

Fortunately, the consensus among employers and career counselors is it doesn't matter what kinds of headings or type styles you use, as long as your resume is easy to read and follows the standard chronological resume form.

Experienced resume reviewers also agree on another point: it's preferable to have a conventional resume as opposed to standing out with a unique format.

"I don't like to see gimmicky things, like bound resumes or resumes in those clear folders," says John Stone, manager of college relations and recruiting programs at Chrysler in Highland Park, Michigan. "The [applicant] is telling me I don't have enough intelligence to determine from the resume if I am interested or not."

Goldman adds, "You want to look sophisticated. Don't have an orange resume."

Putting things in an unusual format in order to catch an employer's eye might make your resume slightly more memorable, but it takes more time for him or her to read it.

Bowen comments, "I prefer a standard layout in a resume. I hire over 400 people a year, and if a resume is totally off base, it takes more time to scan it for the key things I'm looking for."

In addition, unless you're looking for a job in a more visually-oriented field, a wacky resume could look different in a negative way.

"Personnel people are looking for the basics," says Schubert. "You want not to exclude yourself. I would use an unusual format or paper only if applying for an unusual job—something in art or in public relations."

You should also keep in mind how the words are spaced on the page.

"It's good to have a lot of white space and a balanced look, as opposed to something long and cluttered," advises Pavol Bereda.

Goldman strongly urged job hunters to invest in having their resumes professionally typeset.

You can have this done at almost any copy store for under fifty dollars in most large cities. Many typesetters will keep your resume on file, and you can make minor changes periodically for only a few dollars.

The Chronological Resume

Standard chronological resumes start with your name, your address or addresses and your phone numbers. This information is usually centered at the top of the page and is often in bold type.

The body of the chronological resume is marked with the headings we have discussed above. As you've probably figured out from the name, chronological resumes list the relevant things you've done in your life in the order you've done them.

Functional resumes are the other main type of resume. Functional resumes get into groups of skills you have. Rather than flowing in order of time, functional resumes might include some of your college social activities, one or two of your jobs and some course work under a heading like "Leadership Skills."

While functional resumes are acceptable to employers, they're sometimes difficult to read. Unless you've had a lot of work experience, you can end up referring to the same job several times. Even if you've had a lot of work experience, it can be hard for employers to figure out where you worked, when you worked there, and how long you held the job.

Our experts agree that recent college graduates should not get into functional resumes, but should stick to the easy to read and easy to understand chronological format.

"What An - Uh - Interesting Resume"

We've talked about the characteristics of good resumes. It's equally important to remember what makes bad resumes.

Bad resumes have typographical errors. They are vague, cluttered and confusing.

Bad resumes include your weight, height, and the condition of your health. Employers don't really want to know intimate details about your body. If they do, you probably want to look elsewhere.

Bad resumes also include your hobbies. When you include hobbies, it looks as though you didn't have enough to put on your resume. I remember hearing about one guy who listed "laughing" as one of his hobbies. That probably prompted a few snide remarks from people who received his resume, such as "I wonder if he attends laughing seminars" and "do you think he practices his laughs a couple of times a week?"

If you do not have enough to put on your resume, make the margins slightly wider and use a larger typeface. Again, professional typesetters can help you here. It's better to have a sparse resume than one with a lot of unnecessary information.

Bad resumes exaggerate what you've done or boast very weakly about things most people do without thinking about it. For example, I once saw a resume that said, "Perfect class attendance and on-time record."

In general, it's best not to brag about getting out of bed and attending class. If this was such an achievement, this particular job seeker will probably expect some kind of merit award for showing up at work, if she ever finds a job. In addition, unless you're American Airlines, you don't brag about making it someplace on time. You get the idea. Don't put anything on your resume that will make the person reading it wonder if you're being serious.

Now that you've got some ideas for your resume and you've assessed your strong and weak points, you can get started in meeting that goal you set in the last chapter.

Here is a list of steps to take to create an uncommonly successful resume!

Shortening The Distance Between Yourself And Your Goals

1. Write or polish your resume. Use the skills assessment

checklist below, and look at the examples which follow to see how you can get started on, or improve, your resume.

2. Make sure you have enough references. Verify the addresses and phone numbers of those you do have.

3. Have your resume professionally typeset.

4. Make copies of any materials you might send with your resume. For example, if you are seeking a job as a journalist, consider sending writing samples in addition to your resume.

Skills Assessment Checklist

The secret to effective resume writing and interviewing rests not in simply describing your past activities, but in using these activities as part of an organized statement. This statement should tell employers why you would excel in the job they have available and why they should want to hire you. This is a critical concept in job hunting, and an easy one for recent graduates to forget.

For example, when you talk about your participation in student government only in terms of the hours you put in and the meetings you attended, you still haven't persuaded potential employers that there is any reason they should hire you. You haven't set yourself apart from other job hunting candidates.

However, if you describe your participation in student government as a time in which you learned how to organize presentations to be delivered before a large audience and to work with other students who had completely different goals for the school than you did, you've introduced several specific examples of skills which carry over to the workplace. You've demonstrated to potential employers that you'd be an asset to their company.

The following skills assessment guide will help you decide what to include on your resume and how to describe the activities and achievements you include. It will also aid you in putting together your "mental list" of strong points to mention in an interview.

Look over the list and check off any traits that apply to you. Use this as a starting place to recall aspects of your academic courses, summer jobs or collegiate activities which you may have overlooked.

JOB SKILLS REVIEW

Strong academic or work background in particular subject area relevant to job (list here..........................)

Particular hobby which assists in developing skills related to chosen career field (list here...........)

Goal-oriented
Attentive to detail
Good analytical skills
Speak, write or read foreign language
Possess strong written communication skills
Possess strong verbal communication skills
Work well under pressure
Able to receive constructive criticism
Able to give constructive criticism
Tactful in dealing with others
Skilled at:
rapid memorization
retaining facts
meeting deadlines
proofreading and copy editing
presenting polished final document
learning new skills quickly
identifying problems and presenting solutions
carrying through on a project

working independently

working with a group: Specific incident(s) or example

presenting material to a group

motivating others to carry out certain tasks

assisting others in understanding/using new concepts

working with people different from self

organizing thoughts

synthesizing information from a variety of sources

Now, put these traits to work for you on your resume. Think of specific examples from your life which demonstrate the skills you checked off on this list. If you can, fit these examples into the three main categories of your resume: academic achievement, collegiate activities and previous work experience.

• Academic Achievement

Make a list of the strong points of your academic career. Start with the obvious, like a high GPA or serving as a teaching assistant to a graduate student. Next, add on things you might overlook when you're thinking about your college career.

For example, if you took a course out of your field of major because you were interested in the subject, add that to your resume and expand on it in your interview. Perhaps you majored in Latin American Studies, but you took an Economics course on a Pass/Fail basis.

In your interview, explain how taking this course contributed to your academic development. Perhaps it made you think about the link between cultural practices and the economy or it encouraged you to learn more about topics outside your major.

- ## Activities and Community Involvement:

You can and should use your collegiate activities to demonstrate to potential employers that you have the skills for which they're looking.

List the organizations to which you belonged and the contributions you made to these groups. Focus your attention on what it taught you to belong to these groups and how you can carry these skills forward to your first job.

Make sure you don't get bogged down in details, though. If you talk about the sailing club's calendar or the wonders of the yearbook staff's photography lab, and nothing else, you haven't moved from the school to the work environment. Speak proudly of the substance of your activities, but don't stop there.

Instead, describe your ability to lead the sailing club as evidence of your strong interpersonal skills, and link these skills to the job in sales for which you're applying. Equate your experience in the photography lab with an internship in graphic design, and tell a potential employer how you could use your talents to produce a professional looking newsletter for their company.

If you weren't a "joiner" in college, consider making an "activity" out of some of your particular interests or hobbies. If you recycled plastic containers, glass bottles and newspapers during your senior year, and you persuaded one floor of your dorm to do the same, mention it in an interview. Perhaps you typed papers for a fee for a wide circle of friends and acquaintances. Talk about your fledgling "business" and what it taught you about providing a service to demanding clients.

Your recycling efforts and your use of your typing skills certainly won't win you a job, but they can be briefly mentioned as another example of your motivation to make the most of your life and your college experience.

The key to using small, personal examples in your interviews, and, to a lesser extent, on your resume, is to do so honestly and briefly. Just make sure you don't blow these self-initiated activities out of proportion.

Take this time to write a few lines about each of your collegiate activities. Be sure to focus on the skills you learned and think of the specific ways they enhance your qualifications. Just make sure you don't focus solely on the extracurricular activity itself.

• Previous Work Experience

The same holds true for your summer jobs. Play up the specific skills you learned in each job, but stress most strongly the impact a particular job had on your future career goals.

For example, perhaps you worked in a small retail store one summer which was only in its second year of operation. You may immediately think of saying that you learned to operate a cash register...and handle customer complaints...and learn more about direct mail advertising through your assistance with the company catalogue.

What you may not have realized is that it made a big impact on you to see a small business owner in action, and someday you'd like to open your own kite store...or work for a lobbying group in support of small business.

Maybe you worked for a day-care center one summer, and you've realized you'd like a career in which you could contribute to public policy regarding children, either through a job with the government or through a nonprofit organization dedicated to consumer activism.

Just as with your academic experience and your extracurricular activities, the true benefit of your summer jobs is not the tasks you performed, but the way in which the job may have changed your attitudes or helped you enlarge upon your goals.

Finally, don't forget to include on your resume and in your interviews a mention of any technical or interpersonal skills you possess. Check off your qualifications on the list below and add in skills not included on this list.

• Technical Skills:

Familiar with general office environment (list summer jobs here........)

Skilled in writing business letters

Proficient with computer systems and programs (list here.............)

Have experience operating machinery in a factory or plant setting (list here..........)

Qualified to perform CPR and basic first aid

Know how to operate:

    fax machine

    copy machine

    cash register

    travel reservation system

    audio visual equipment

    photography equipment

    Other:

• Interpersonal Skills:

Comfortable in new situations

Enjoy meeting new people

Enjoy taking on new responsibilities

Confident

Enthusiastic about projects in which involved

Interested in achieving new goals

Friendly

Flexible
Stable
Easy to get along with
Loyal to organizations in which involved
Skilled at:
    expressing own opinions confidently
    listening to others' opinions even when they differ
      from own
    compromising with others in order to reach goals
    acting as mediator or resolving disputes between people
      or groups
    making new contacts within other organizations

Now that you're armed with specific examples which clearly demonstrate your strong points, you can feel comfortable talking about your excellent academic record or your strong interpersonal skills.

Mention these points on your resume, in your cover letters and in your interviews, and you'll find yourself in the midst of a successful and productive job search!

Sample Resumes

SUSAN HALLEY
11418 WESTERN CIRCLE COURT
OMAHA, NEBRASKA 68137
(402) 333-3333

EDUCATION:
Dartmouth University
Hanover, New Hampshire
B.S. in Economics, 1992, Summa Cum Laude. Grade Point Average: 3.9.
Relevant coursework: Principles of Accounting; Advanced Microeconomic
Theory; Industrial Economics and Public Policy.

WORK EXPERIENCE:
Summer Intern
Price Waterhouse, San Francisco, California
Summer 1991
Conducted economic research; built charts on Macintosh for monthly
client report. Assisted project manager with new business development
by writing background material on Price Waterhouse projects and staff.
One of ten interns selected from 120 applicants.

Summer Intern
Thompson Construction Company, Omaha, Nebraska
Summer 1990
Worked for accountant in five person company. Created spread sheets
using Lotus 1-2-3. Improved company's late payment collection procedure by drafting series of overdue notices. Coordinated telephone calls
and payment penalties with collection agencies.

Summer Sales Person
The Gap, Omaha, Nebraska
Summer, 1987, 1988, 1989.
Handled all merchandise returns and exchanges, worked in stock room,
operated sophisticated cash register and electronic credit card checking
device. During last two summers, assisted manager in opening and
closing store. Received Gap Employee-of-the-Month award for emphasis
on customer service.

COLLEGIATE ACTIVITIES:
Chairman, Senior Gifts Campaign, 1991-1992
Directed program encouraging members of senior class to pledge gifts for coming years. Received highest pledge offering in past five years based on innovative system of flyers to dorm rooms.
President, Honor Council, 1990-1991
Implemented new judicial system for investigating Honor Code violations. Developed survey of student body, presented findings to administration and alumni board, won adoption of new procedures for determining punishment of Honor Code violators.
Member, Dartmouth Players, 1990-1992.
Aerobics Instructor, 1988-1992.

TECHNICAL SKILLS:
Proficient in Macintosh, Wordstar, WordPerfect.

References available upon request

MICHAEL PATTERSON
1252 DIRABEAUX DRIVE
NEW ORLEANS, LOUISIANA 70122
(504) 333-3333

OBJECTIVE:
a) To utilize my interpersonal and sales skills to work in corporate fund-raising.
b) To work as a translator of documents written in Russian. Particular interest in translating and developing sales and marketing materials for companies interested in operating within the Soviet Union.

EDUCATIONAL BACKGROUND:
Illinois State University
Normal, Illinois
B.A. Russian Studies; 1992. Grade Point Average: 2.6.
Minor, Fine Arts.
Selected Course Work in Major: Russian Civilization; Advanced Russian Syntax; Topics in Russian Literature. Selected Course Work in Minor: Survey of Art; Arts and the Modern World.

PROFESSIONAL EXPERIENCE:
Illinois State University
Office of Undergraduate Admissions
Normal, Illinois
1988-1992
Spoke to large groups of potential students; organized and scheduled student tours. Assisted in production of catalogues on university and academic life with desktop publishing. Used earnings to pay for one-fourth of college tuition.

Department of Russian Studies
Summer Art History Travel Program
Summer 1992
Traveled to ten different cities in the Soviet Union. Achieved fluency in Russian; wrote paper on Soviet contributions to 19th century art.

Full-time Summer Intern
Art Institute of Chicago
Chicago, Illinois
Summer 1991
Served as intern in Institute's Cultural Diversity program. Attended daily lectures. Topics included impact of political climate on artistic expression. Assisted curator with exhibit set-up, data entry and general office work. Called previous patrons to solicit donations.

Part-time cook
Big Al's Burger and Fries
Chicago, Illinois
Summer 1991
Worked as cook on nights and weekends at neighborhood restaurant in order to participate in unpaid museum internship.

Summer Sales Assistant
Antiques & Ornaments
New Orleans, Louisiana
Summers, 1989, 1990
Worked as summer sales assistant for antique store. Assisted with monthly inventory process, advised clients on purchases. Initiated new method of tracking clients' purchasing patterns and notifying them when similar pieces arrived in store.

COLLEGIATE ACTIVITIES:
President, Fine Arts Council, 1991-1992. Oversaw annual student art show. Increased show attendance by 25 percent by advertising at local art stores and galleries.
Captain, Intramural Football Team, 1990-91.

NOTEWORTHY ACHIEVEMENT:
Volunteer Translator, 1990-1992
During junior and senior years, volunteered as translator for recent Soviet immigrants. Recognized by YMCA's Relocation Service for "contribution and commitment" to program.

HAL SIMMS
532 LAKEWOOD LOOP
LANCASTER, PENNSYLVANIA 17602
(717) 333-3333

OBJECTIVE:
To use my programming and troubleshooting experience and my knowledge of telecommunications to work in management systems. To develop my career to eventually manage several other individuals in a technical environment.

EDUCATION:
University of California, Irvine, California
B.S., 1992, Information and Computer Science. GPA: 3.6
Related coursework: Principles of Operating Systems; Programming Languages; Introduction to Software Engineering.

WORK HISTORY:
Summer Intern
RMV Systems Management, Inc.
Lancaster, Pennsylvania
Summer, 1991
Developed internal software tracking system for RMV Systems, a systems integrator with focus on telecommunications. Went on maintenance calls with lead analyst. Interacted with clients to identify problems and present solutions.

Waiter
The Cadillac Cafe
Lancaster, Pennsylvania
Summers, 1989, 1990
Worked as waiter for large restaurant. Handled special events; worked with beverage and food distributors to coordinate deliveries.

COLLEGIATE ACTIVITIES:
Resident Advisor, 1990-1991
Oversaw coed freshman dorm housing 250 students. Responsible for organizing dorm social events; overseeing dorm elections; scheduling shifts of student security officers at front entrance; general oversight of student's needs during first year away from home. As result of this leadership position, learned to manage and direct others; mediate disputes; communicate effectively.

SPECIAL ACHIEVEMENT:
Served as consultant to RMV Systems after conclusion of internship. Called back to company several times to catch flaws in new software system; paid retainer's fee during final semester of college.
1991-1992

MEMBERSHIP IN PROFESSIONAL ORGANIZATIONS:
Member, Association of Computer and Engineering Students, 1988-1992

References available

Notes on Sample Resumes

SUSAN HALLEY
11418 WESTERN CIRCLE COURT
OMAHA, NEBRASKA 68137
(402) 333-3333

Note: Susan is sending her resume to Big Six accounting firms and to accountants in smaller firms. Given her course work and summer job experience, her career goals are clear, and she therefore can omit the objective. If your career goals will be equally obvious to the potential employers to whom you send your resume, you can omit the objective also.

EDUCATION:
Dartmouth University
Hanover, New Hampshire
B.S. in Economics, 1992, Summa Cum Laude. Grade Point Average: 3.9.
Relevant coursework: Principles of Accounting; Advanced Microeconomic Theory; Industrial Economics and Public Policy.

Note: Susan's high GPA becomes all the more impressive after she lists several difficult courses on her resume. If you took some challenging classes, and you did well, include them on your resume.

WORK EXPERIENCE:
Summer Intern
Price Waterhouse, San Francisco, California
Summer 1991

Conducted economic research; built charts on Macintosh for monthly client report. Assisted project manager with new business development by writing background material on Price Waterhouse projects and staff. One of ten interns selected from 120 applicants.

Note: Susan gives a context to her job activities. In saying that the background materials she wrote were used to seek new business, she stresses the importance of what she did. If she had simply said she wrote background materials, her resume would not be as effective. She also uses specific details to demonstrate how competitive it was to win the internship.

Summer Intern
Thompson Construction Company, Omaha, Nebraska
Summer 1990

Worked for accountant in five person company. Created spread sheets using Lotus 1-2-3. Improved company's late payment collection procedure by drafting series of overdue notices. Coordinated telephone calls and payment penalties with collection agencies.

Note: Susan gives concrete examples of what she has accomplished in each part of her resume. Here, she takes credit for improving one aspect of her employer's business, and she tells exactly how she made that improvement. You can do the same, whether you updated your summer employer's phone log or simplified a form used for customer complaints.

Summer Sales Person
The Gap, Omaha, Nebraska

Summer, 1987, 1988, 1989.
Handled all merchandise returns and exchanges, worked in stock room, operated sophisticated cash register and electronic credit card checking device. During last two summers, assisted manager in opening and closing store. Received Gap Employee-of-the-Month award for emphasis on customer service.

COLLEGIATE ACTIVITIES:
Chairman, Senior Gifts Campaign, 1991-1992
Directed program encouraging members of senior class to pledge gifts for coming years. Received highest pledge offering in past five years based on innovative system of flyers to dorm rooms.

Note: Susan clearly states her major accomplishment, that of achieving the highest pledge commitment, and she gives details on how she reached that goal.

President, Honor Council, 1990-1991
Implemented new judicial system for investigating Honor Code violations. Developed survey of student body, presented findings to administration and alumni board, won adoption of new procedures for determining punishment of Honor Code violators.
Member, Dartmouth Players, 1990-1992.
Aerobics Instructor, 1988-1992.

TECHNICAL SKILLS:
Proficient in Macintosh, Wordstar, WordPerfect.

References available upon request

MICHAEL PATTERSON
1252 DIRABEAUX DRIVE
NEW ORLEANS, LOUISIANA 70122
(504) 333-3333

OBJECTIVE:
a) To utilize my interpersonal and sales skills to work in corporate fund-raising.
b) To work as a translator of documents written in Russian. Particular interest in translating and developing sales and marketing materials for companies interested in operating within the Soviet Union.

Note: Because Michael is a liberal arts major looking for a job in a variety of fields, he has several different resumes. The body of each resume is the same, but the objectives differ. Obviously, he only uses one objective on each resume, and in this way gives potential employers a clear idea of his career goals.

EDUCATIONAL BACKGROUND:
Illinois State University
Normal, Illinois
B.A. Russian Studies; 1992. Grade Point Average: 2.6.
Minor, Fine Arts.
Selected Course Work in Major: Russian Civilization; Advanced Russian Syntax; Topics in Russian Literature. Selected Course Work in Minor: Survey of Art; Arts and the Modern World.

PROFESSIONAL EXPERIENCE:
Illinois State University
Office of Undergraduate Admissions

59

Normal, Illinois
1988-1992
Spoke to large groups of potential students; organized and scheduled student tours. Assisted in production of catalogues on university and academic life with desktop publishing. Used earnings to pay for one-fourth of college tuition.

Note: Career counselors and employers recommend you mention any financial contributions you made to your college education. Michael's steady part-time work, coming on top of a full load of classes, shows drive and commitment. This is also a good way to make up for a lower GPA.

Department of Russian Studies
Summer Art History Travel Program
Summer 1992
Traveled to ten different cities in the Soviet Union. Achieved fluency in Russian; wrote paper on Soviet contributions to 19th century art.

Note: In stating his achievements, such as fluency in the language and the completion of a paper, Michael sets this trip apart from a casual sight-seeing venture. If you did something interesting, whether it was travel or an internship, point out the substantive things you accomplished. This is especially important if it sounds as though it was something that you did only for fun.

Full-time Summer Intern
Art Institute of Chicago
Chicago, Illinois
Summer 1991

Served as intern in Institute's Cultural Diversity program. Attended daily lectures. Topics included impact of political climate on artistic expression. Assisted curator with exhibit set-up, data entry and general office work. Called previous patrons to solicit donations.

Part-time cook
Big Al's Burger and Fries
Chicago, Illinois
Summer 1991

Worked as cook on nights and weekends at neighborhood restaurant in order to participate in unpaid museum internship.

Note: Taking on a tedious part-time job in order to participate in a prestigious and equally demanding summer internship demonstrates ambition and a willingness to work to get ahead. If you worked a menial job in order to finance your education or even your violin lessons, put that on your resume. It gives a little more insight into you as a person and sets you apart from other job seekers.

Summer Sales Assistant
Antiques & Ornaments
New Orleans, Louisiana
Summers, 1989, 1990
Worked as summer sales assistant for antique store. Assisted with monthly inventory process, advised clients on purchases. Initiated new method of tracking clients' purchasing patterns and notifying them when similar pieces arrived in store.

Note: In letting customers know about antiques which they would be likely to purchase, Michael demonstrated his business acumen and his people skills. If you did something in your job which revealed a clear understanding of your employers' goals, include this on your resume.

For example, maybe one of your summer employers was focused on cutting costs, and you found a cheaper source for staplers than the one the company was currently using. The action itself was small, but it reveals that you can further the interests of the organizations you work for.

COLLEGIATE ACTIVITIES:
President, Fine Arts Council, 1991-1992. Oversaw annual student art show. Increased show attendance by 25 percent by advertising at local art stores and galleries.
Captain, Intramural Football Team, 1990-91.

Note: Even though Michael does not have a high GPA, he still has a good resume. This is because he uses his part-time job, interesting activities and summer travel experiences to compensate for his low grades.

NOTEWORTHY ACHIEVEMENT:
Volunteer Translator, 1990-1992
During junior and senior years, volunteered as translator for recent Soviet immigrants. Recognized by YMCA's Relocation Service for "contribution and commitment" to program.

Note: This is a good way to use the special achievements category, especially if your award is an informal one that wouldn't immediately come to mind (or wouldn't fit under any other category on your resume).

HAL SIMMS
532 LAKEWOOD LOOP
LANCASTER, PENNSYLVANIA 17602
(717) 333-3333

OBJECTIVE:
To use my programming and troubleshooting experience and my knowledge of telecommunications to work in management systems. To develop my career to eventually manage several other individuals in a technical environment.

Note: Hal uses the objective to point out his experience in and knowledge of the computer industry, but, as career counselors stress, he isn't using "overblown" language. His objective is matter-of-fact and to the point.

EDUCATION:
University of California, Irvine, California
B.S., 1992, Information and Computer Science. GPA: 3.6
Related coursework: Principles of Operating Systems; Programming Languages; Introduction to Software Engineering.

Note: As you can see, this resume says "related" coursework, and the other two samples say "relevant" and "selected." There are a lot of different ways to phrase things on your resume. As long as you use clear, concise language, you can use whatever words sound best to you.

WORK HISTORY:
Summer Intern
RMV Systems Management, Inc.
Lancaster, Pennsylvania
Summer, 1991
Developed internal software tracking system for RMV Systems, a systems integrator with focus on telecommunications. Went on maintenance calls with lead analyst. Interacted with clients to identify problems and present solutions.

Note: Hal points out that he helped clients solve problems. Whether you solved problems, helped to create a product or contributed to an employee newsletter, be sure to state the results of your efforts. The most important part of your resume is not what you did, but the results your actions achieved.

Waiter
The Cadillac Cafe
Lancaster, Pennsylvania
Summers, 1989, 1990
Worked as waiter for large restaurant. Handled special events; worked with beverage and food distributors to coordinate deliveries.

Note: Hal stresses his interaction with other people and his additional responsibilities, but he doesn't try to gloss over the fact that he was a waiter. Be proud of your summer jobs. The only thing to keep in mind is that you need to describe them truthfully.

COLLEGIATE ACTIVITIES:
Resident Advisor, 1990-1991

Oversaw coed freshman dorm housing 250 students. Responsible for organizing dorm social events; overseeing dorm elections; scheduling shifts of student security officers at front entrance; general oversight of student's needs during first year away from home. As result of this leadership position, learned to manage and direct others; mediate disputes; communicate effectively.

Note: This is a good example of being able to see the importance behind your activities and describing them in a way that gives employers a glimpse into your work habits. Clearly, Hal has had some experience in trying to get people to get along with each other, and he can carry these skills over to his first job out of college.

SPECIAL ACHIEVEMENT:
Served as consultant to RMV Systems after conclusion of internship. Called back to company several times to catch flaws in new software system; paid retainer's fee during final semester of college.
1991-1992

Note: This could be listed on Hal's resume under his description of the job itself. It is such an outstanding achievement, however, that it has more impact when listed separately.

MEMBERSHIP IN PROFESSIONAL ORGANIZA-TIONS:
Member, Association of Computer and Engineering Students, 1988-1992

References available

DIFFERENTIATING YOUR RESUME WITH THE PERFECT COVER LETTER... I Don't Remember Seeing Anything About Cover Letters In Cliffs' Notes

"Discovery consists of looking at the same thing as everyone else and thinking something different."
—Albert Szent-Gyorgyi

By sending a well-written cover letter with your resume, you can differentiate yourself and assist employers in "discovering" you.

Cover letters are essential. They're sort of like the first project or paper you turn in to a professor in that they go a long way in contributing to that first impression you make on a potential employer.

"I recommend every resume have a cover letter," says career

counselor Susan Schubert of Schubert & Associates. "The cover letter acts as a bridge between the applicant and the resume."

The cover letter demonstrates your interest in a company and your desire to work there, and it influences the way employers perceive your application.

"I don't feel warmly about resumes without cover letters," says John Stone, manager of college relations and recruiting programs at Chrysler. "I do look at them, but I don't see them as serious attempts."

Writing an effective cover letter requires thought, skill and planning. It also requires an overall sense of direction. You need to know why you're writing a cover letter and what you expect to get out of it.

As we discussed in the chapter on resumes, employers want to know why they should hire you. They want to know enough about you as a person to be able to answer that critical question: "What distinguishes you from other candidates?"

Answering this question for employers is the primary reason for writing a cover letter. You want to sell yourself and your abilities. You want to highlight the strongest points on your resume and point out special achievements.

As one career counselor explains it, cover letters provide you with another opportunity to promote yourself.

"A cover letter is crucial as your own marketing tool," says career counselor Marilyn Goldman of Horizons Unlimited. "The cover letter is a restatement of your resume in a different format."

The cover letter also tells employers in very specific terms exactly the type of job for which you're looking. That sounds basic, but your major and your resume don't always reflect the type of job you want or the type you will end up with down the road. Did I hear a sigh of relief from all those Anthropology and Spanish Studies majors?

If you have a liberal arts degree, you can pursue a wide variety of careers. It can be difficult for busy employers to know exactly what you're looking for simply from your resume. Here's where the cover letter makes a difference. From your cover letter, employers learn where to steer your resume or where to file it if there aren't any jobs available in that area at a given time.

"A cover letter is important," comments Terri Goslin-Jones, director of employment at Perpetual Bank. "Without one, we don't know where to forward a resume."

What's In A Cover Letter?

A cover letter, like any other letter, includes an introduction, a body and a closing. The introduction explains who you are, what you want and why you're writing the letter.

The body describes your background and experiences and states why you are well-suited for the job you're seeking.

The closing gives you a chance to take an active role and tell the employer when you will be back in touch.

The cover letter follows the basic business letter format. Of course, even the best summer jobs don't include a lot of business letter writing, so don't be discouraged if it takes a little time for you to master the layout of a business letter. This chapter will help you feel a lot more comfortable with the style.

How Long Is A Cover Letter?

One of the first dilemmas when you start to write anything is determining the length. In general, the shorter your cover letter, the better.

I remember when I wrote my first "real" cover letter. It was for a summer internship in Washington, D.C. while I was still a sophomore in college, so I guess I can use lack of experience as an excuse for writing what I now realize was the most pathetic attempt at a business letter anyone has ever seen.

Being a novice to the business letter concept, I thought you had to give the person you were writing your basic life history before you really got into the meat of the topic. You don't want to rush into anything.

I started the letter by introducing myself. While introductions are necessary to some extent, I pretty much gave a life summary in the opening paragraph. I told them where I went to school and how I came to select that school.

Several pages later, I got around to explaining that I'd like to apply for an internship if they didn't mind.

This was after explaining at length why I wanted to spend the summer in Washington (I couldn't face the dismal boredom of a dry, hot summer in my hometown), why I was interested in this particular internship (a lot of people from my school had similar internships every summer) and how I thought I would benefit from the experience (who doesn't benefit from having a great summer job?).

I had the right idea, and I was selected for the internship, but I went a little overboard with the background. So, to avoid a similar source of future embarrassment, keep your cover letters short.

The opening should be a one or two sentence paragraph. The body can range from two to four paragraphs. It's the heart of your cover letter, and it takes up the most space. The closing paragraph is roughly the same length as the opening, perhaps one or two sentences.

Cover letters should never be longer than one page. According to one career counselor, an overly long cover letter is one of the first places an applicant loses points in job hunting.

"Your cover letter should be brief and to the point," explains General Electric's Peter Bowen. "It shouldn't be five pages long."

"What Do I Talk About In A Cover Letter?"

There are two schools of thought as to what you should focus on in your cover letter.

Some career counselors and employers think you should talk mostly about yourself, explaining why you're the best person for the job. Others believe you should talk mostly about the employer, referring to their needs and demonstrating what you know about the company.

Successful cover letters contain a little bit of both approaches. I recommend writing primarily about yourself, because writing about the employer requires considerable time and research.

You probably don't have time to do extensive research. Fortunately, you can wage an equally successful and productive job hunt even if you keep in-depth research on potential employers to a minimum. Of course, many employers are offended by a letter that's clearly part of a mass mailing you sent to 500 or so of your favorite companies.

"A cover letter shouldn't give the sense it is addressed to "Dear Occupant," explains Stone.

Just as you discard a lot of the junk mail that comes your way, employers frequently have the nerve to take the same attitude toward the piece of art that is your cover letter. You therefore need to find a balance between making each cover letter so unique that you have no time to do anything but write cover letters, and making each cover letter so generic that employers immediately discard them.

Luckily, there are a lot of employers who want to hear about you, rather than about what you think their company needs.

"I prefer to see a student use a cover letter to show me what he or she has done in a job or community experience as opposed to what the student can do for Ford," says Ford's Darrell Washington.

To the time-conscious job hunter, that's good news. Not only is it easier to talk about your skills, it can appear presumptuous to talk about what a company needs. Unless you've spent a significant amount of time reading about a company and you have a background in business or marketing, you probably don't really know what it needs. If you write a letter that talks about the company and you're not quite on target, you will likely lose the chance to interview there.

"Let Me Introduce Myself"

The first section of the cover letter tells exactly why you're writing the employer and what it is you're looking for.

You want to convince employers to read your letter and to look at your resume. Therefore, you need to slip the first positive reference to yourself into the opening paragraph.

For example, it's better to say:

"I recently graduated from the University of Alaska with a 4.0 in engineering, and I would like to work in your plastics manufacturing plant"

than to say:

"I am writing in response to your ad in the Daily Tribune for engineers to work in your plastics manufacturing plant. I recently graduated from college, and I am interested in working for your company."

As you promote yourself, try to give the employers only the

bare facts. Don't get bogged down with details as to how you learned about the job or where you saw it advertised. The distinction between the first and second openings is subtle, but it sets the tone for your entire letter. Think of every sentence of the cover letter as an opportunity not only for you to tell the employers what you want, but for you to tell the employers why they should want you.

I know, your clear mastery of college social life and your impressive roster of upper level courses should be enough to satisfy anyone, but these employers can be slow. You've therefore got to reiterate your strong points.

In the example above, the accomplishment to which you refer in the first sentence is portrayed more vividly when you open your letter with it than when you wait for three paragraphs to mention it.

Perhaps your GPA wasn't that great, so you can't refer to it in your opening sentence, but you've worked for three summers at Yellowstone National Park. You're now looking for a job with an environmental issues lobbying group.

Rather than saying:

"I have always been interested in wildlife preservation, and I would like to work in the position you advertised,"

you could say:

"I am interested in working as a staff consultant with your organization, and I believe the three summers I spent working on preservation issues at Yellowstone National Park qualifies me for the job you have available."

Unfortunately, not every job for which you apply ties in with your own experiences. Of course, a lot of unqualified people seem to do just fine in their jobs, but that's probably not a good argument. If your life history doesn't match up with the job you want, keep the opening of your cover letter short so you can move rapidly to discussing your skills in the body of the letter.

You can see now that the opening paragraph is essential. If you begin in the right vein, you can use the opening paragraph to set yourself apart from other candidates.

"I'm Just The Person You're Looking For—Really!"

The second section of your cover letter, the body, gives specific examples to illustrate why you're a good candidate for the job.

The body of the letter should only have three or four main thoughts outlined in three or four paragraphs. The fact that you'd pay them to hire you probably shouldn't be included.

The body may have one paragraph on a job you've held and one on an honor or award you've won. In this section, you can pick up where you left off in the opening paragraph. For example, if you've already mentioned a specific job, talent or academic experience, develop it more fully here.

Give yourself two or three sentences to say what was significant about that experience and how it relates to the job for which you're applying.

If you haven't gotten into anything specific yet, this is the place to do it. Of course, you probably thought you had a pretty exciting life until you tried to write about it in a cover letter.

Fortunately, even if you didn't make the cover of Time magazine at a young age, you can still write an interesting cover letter about yourself and your abilities.

Writing an exciting cover letter requires you to relate your skills to the job for which you're applying, whether you acquired these skills through an impressive internship or through some mundane college experience. For example, your starring role in a college play or your involvement with student government, do not, on the surface, appear relevant to your hopes for a career in banking.

If you can mention that the skills you learned in the theater make you a better business person or that your tenure as vice president of the student government association taught you how to motivate those working for you, you've related your abilities to what the employers are looking for. And you haven't had to stretch too hard to do it.

Often, employers filling entry level positions with recent college graduates don't really care how applicants developed their talent. They just care that applicants have the necessary skills. Most employers are interested in all aspects of your collegiate experience, and will take you seriously even if you need to discuss extracurricular activities to demonstrate your abilities.

Ford's Washington says, "I encourage students to show they've been involved. When we see someone who was the president of some kind of student organization, that is a good sign. We're looking for leadership."

This is true of most employers. However, there are some cases where talking about the college tennis team or your enthusiasm for adventure aren't sufficient. If you can't make your activities relate to the job in some way, don't force it. This is one part of writing cover letters that trips up a lot of recent graduates.

"Don't try to torture a connection," advises Dr. Ray Harrison of Manchester. "When students respond to an ad to sell nuclear submarines and talk about their experience waiting tables, it's a mismatch between their experience and their objectives."

Harrison suggested you talk about your sincere interest in the industry and your commitment to learning more about a particular field.

"I'm Looking Forward To Talking To You"

The third section of your cover letter gives you a chance to take a more active role in the job hunting process. You should always tell employers you will get back in touch with them, and then do that when you said you would.

For example, you might say "Thank you for considering my resume. I will call your office next week, and I look forward to speaking to you then if you are available."

It's best to state a time frame, like one week, and to give them enough time to assimilate the information from all of the resumes they've received.

I've found it to be very effective to say I would call employers and then subsequently call them, as promised. Frequently, potential employers would say they were glad I had the initiative to follow up on the letter I sent them. This can work for you too.

Surprisingly, a lot of job seekers don't make any effort to follow up on the letters they send out, and this is a critical step. Saying you will follow up and then doing that gives you one more way to stand out from the crowd of job hunters.

Of course, some employers either won't take your call or won't ever call you back. It's a good rule of thumb to call employers, give them a day or two to call you back and then try again once or twice.

If you place two or three calls over the space of a week and never receive a return phone call, give up on that employer and use your time to do something more productive.

As a recent college graduate, it's hard to pick up on these unspoken rules of business. It's difficult to know where to draw the line between impressing employers with your ambition and driving them crazy with your unwanted persistence.

However, if employers will take your call, you can achieve a lot with one phone call, so be sure to mention in your cover letter that you'll be calling.

As you close your cover letter, mention that you have references who can recommend you. You can also say if you are enclosing anything with your resume.

Now that you've figured out the format of the cover letter, it's time to figure out how to write it.

Putting It All Together

Some job hunters get stuck when they sit down and start working on their cover letters. They know what they want to say, but they can't get it to sound right. Does this remind you of all those papers you wrote?

So they'll write a few sentences, scribble them out or delete them, and a few hours later they're still sitting there with nothing written because it all sounds wrong.

The solution is to get your thoughts on paper and to not worry about how it sounds. Sit down and hammer out a page, whether it's for a cover letter or a thank you note, and put in everything you want to say.

Don't worry if it doesn't flow, if it's filled with grammatical errors, or if it isn't phrased well.

No matter how bad this very rough draft sounds, go ahead and forge through the whole letter. Whatever you do, don't write a few sentences and then scribble them out or delete them.

If what you've written makes sense and has some logical order, you're now ready to rewrite each part until it reads smoothly.

If it doesn't have any logical order and looks like a lot of disconnected thoughts, that's probably where your problem lies. You can't get it to sound right because you aren't really sure what you're trying to say. In this case, go back to square one and determine what the main thought is for each paragraph. Once you're clear on what you want to say in each paragraph, you can breeze through the actual writing of your letter.

This might sound haphazard or time-consuming, but you can always polish what you have on a page. You can't do anything with a blank page or blank screen, and it's amazing how much time you can spend sitting there.

"I Write Form Letters to All Of My Closest Friends"

Now that you've tackled your first version of the cover letter, you need to decide how much time you can afford to spend on each subsequent letter. Should you send in the same letter in response to every ad? Or should you write a new letter each time you find a new job opportunity?

The realistic job hunter will send out hundreds of cover letters for a variety of jobs which are all built upon the same set of skills. The challenge lies in writing form letters that look as though they were written in specific response to one ad.

As we've already discussed, employers don't like it when you're clearly sending them a letter which you've sent to fifty other companies in response to ads they've posted. However, you don't have to write fifty different letters for fifty different jobs. All you need is to write a letter that fits in with the job you're seeking and accomplishes the end result of differentiating your resume and snaring you an interview. If you can develop two or three letters which you can alter slightly to answer fifty ads, you've mastered the whole cover letter game.

"Did You See That Ad For The Gamekeeper In Kenya?"

Unfortunately, some great job always comes up that doesn't fit in with your cover letters in any way.

In some cases, it's because the job is in a narrow area. Or because the employer wants someone with the ability to cope with very specific responsibilities.

To show that you're the right one for the job, you need to make some mention of the qualities for which they're looking. You also need a few sentences telling how great you are in exactly that area.

This is frustrating because coming up with those few sentences can take half an hour. Working them into the letter requires shifting paragraphs around. Pretty soon you have basically rewritten your entire letter and spent an hour in the process.

The 24 Hour Question

Clearly, you need to decide how much time you want to devote to an individual letter. Often, ads that look as though they require very individual responses could be answered well with one of your form letters. They could probably best be answered with an individual letter, but you do not have time to respond that way to all of the ads you see.

When you need a very personalized letter, you need to set priorities. Does the job requiring the individual letter look like a great job you'd love to have, or is it just one more thing from the newspaper on which you ought to follow up?

Decide how much you want this job. I know, you want any job. But it'll save you a lot of frustration if you keep your time spent personalizing cover letters to a minimum, because you may not hear back on a lot of the letters you send out.

So if a job looks like it was tailor-made for you, and it's everything you were looking for, go ahead and spend some extra time on the cover letter. But if it looks like it would be an average job or it's not in an area you really care about, be a little more selective with your time.

There's nothing worse than working for hours on what seems to be the perfect cover letter, never to hear from the company at all, or never to have your phone calls returned.

It's also disappointing to look back through your files and see cover letters you thought were incredible that don't really seem all that jazzy on a second reading.

Cover letters are a very important part of the job search. You can use them to get an advantage over other candidates, but it's self-defeating to spend too much time on any one job response.

A One Of A Kind Cover Letter For A Once In A Lifetime Opportunity

However, some jobs you see advertised will look so great you've just got to send in the perfect cover letter. In that case, follow these pointers.

One way to revise your letter quickly is to keep in mind the basic points you want to get across. It's easy to get bogged down in all of the specifics of the job and then to get off on a tangent.

Maybe that summer you spent as a camp counselor really did change your life in some way, but the more you discuss the things you learned in any one experience, the more work you have to do to relate this back to the job you're seeking. In other words, the further you get from your basic form letter, the longer it'll take you to write the response.

To keep yourself focused, keep a very close watch on the changes you make and on the time you allot yourself to make these changes. For example, tell yourself you can spend fifteen minutes making your form letter match up to the job for which you're applying, and be very strict about the changes you make. Retain the basic body of your form letter and simply refer to the specific job two or three times throughout the letter.

If the advertisement calls for someone who has had management experience, add in only one sentence at the end of your paragraph about how you supervised others during a summer job.

For example, instead of trying to develop a cohesive paragraph about management skills and your experience, write one or two sentences to add on to the basic paragraph in which you mention your other skills.

"What A Great Looking Cover Letter"

When you walked across that stage and got your diploma, you probably didn't expect to spend your time analyzing such things as paper stock and type fonts. However, little details in your cover letter can make a difference, and the physical appearance of your cover letter is important.

If you're lucky enough to be using a computer, it's important to send out cover letters that are printed in "letter quality" or "near-letter quality" type.

These terms refer to the way your computer prints on the page. Letter-quality simply means the letters are completely inked in, and the type looks like that of any regular book or magazine you would read. Letter-quality printing is preferable, as it's easier to read and it looks better on the page.

Near-letter quality type encompasses a wide range of printing styles. Some near-letter quality printers are so close to letter-quality that they look completely inked in and are easy to read. The problem comes when you use a near-letter quality printer that makes each letter look like it is a fuzzy mixture of little dots (which is actually how the words are typed).

Near-letter quality type looks like something you'd print out at the computer room at school, and it's often difficult to read.

If you don't have access to a letter-quality printer, you also might consider photocopying your letters onto a higher quality paper, such as a white bond. Your letters will look more attractive and more professional, but, of course, this is more expensive than using regular paper. You need to see what will fit into your budget, but in general, the more attractive the appearance of your cover letter and your resume, the more likely they are to make a favorable impression on an employer.

It might take a lot of cover letters to get a few interested responses from employers, but don't let that bother you. Once you master the basics, sending out cover letters can be a painless procedure. And as soon as you write your basic cover letter, you're ready to get into the exciting part: contacting and meeting with potential employers! We'll discuss this in the next chapter.

Want To Be Discovered? Follow These Tips!

1. Take an hour or two to make all of the decisions regarding your cover letter. What are the main work experiences to which you will refer? What are some of your more desirable personal qualities?

You can think of abstract things here, like saying you're a good leader, an assertive speaker, articulate, well-organized, work well under pressure, etc. How did your academic work contribute to your growth? What are your special accomplishments? Decide how these things can be threaded together to make a cohesive cover letter.

2. Write a basic cover letter. Use the following examples to help yourself get started, and set a deadline by which you'll complete the letter. A good time frame might be three days.

As we mentioned in the first chapter, you can alternate writing your cover letter with working on your resume. Try to finish both within two weeks. You might decide you will have the rough draft of your cover letter finished within three days of starting it. You can spend the remaining time rewording it, improving the sentence structure and eliminating unnecessary phrases.

3. Determine where you will send your cover letter and resume. To get some ideas, read the next chapter.

Sample Cover Letters

Date

Mr. X
Big Six Accounting Firm
City, State, Zip

Dear Mr. X:

I recently graduated from Dartmouth University with a 3.9 in Economics, and I would like to work on your staff. Given my summer internships, both for Price Waterhouse and for a small construction company, and my ability to work well as part of a team, I believe I am qualified for the position you have available.

At Price Waterhouse, I assisted in preparing proposals to attract new clients. In doing this, I learned how to tailor information to the needs of potential customers, and I learned how to conduct a thorough follow-up campaign.

In working for a small construction company under the direct supervision of the lead accountant, I learned how to schedule and complete the daily assignments which keep a business running smoothly. I would like to utilize and build on this experience for (name of accounting firm), and I hope I will have an opportunity to work for you.

I am adept at selling a group on an idea and motivating those I work with to accomplish clearly defined goals. For example, under my leadership, Dartmouth's senior gifts campaign brought in more money for the school than it had at any time in the previous five years. I could not have accomplished this without a strong gifts committee, but I believe my organization of our fund-raising efforts and my willingness to listen to - and implement - new ideas contributed greatly to our success.

Sincerely,

Susan Halley

Sarah Hart

Date

Ms. Y
International Business Consulting Firm
City, State, Zip

Dear Ms. Y:

I am seeking a position in which I can use my fluency in Russian and my knowledge of sales, and I am writing to request an interview at your convenience.

I have strong language skills. In addition to my coursework in Russian Studies, I gained "hands on" experience as a volunteer translator for Russian immigrants during my junior and senior years. In this role, I learned more about Soviet language and culture, and I also learned more about myself and my own values. I believe it is crucial for Soviet and American companies to understand something of each other's history, culture and outlook, and I can bring this knowledge to the job.

I am also adept at sales, whether I am selling a concept or a product. For example, I worked to "sell" Illinois State University through my job with the undergraduate admissions office. I conducted tours for groups of high school students who were considering attending the University. Each year, approximately twenty to twenty-five freshman would tell me that my style of describing the University and campus life had made a difference to them the previous spring when they had selected the college they would attend.

Through my summer job with a specialized antique store, I have also learned how to sell a product. As part of my job, I worked to develop client relationships, and I learned the value of listening to customers to determine their goals.

I hope I will have an opportunity to use my academic background and my challenging work experiences in a position at (company name). I will call your office in two weeks, and I look forward to talking to you then if you are available.

Sincerely,

Michael Patterson

Date

Mr. Z
Fortune 100 Computer Manufacturing Company
City, State, Zip

Dear Mr. Z:

I can offer (name of company) a solid background in telecommunications and software engineering as well as strong interpersonal skills. My name is Hal Simms, and I'd like to be the next addition to your staff.

During my senior year, I served as a paid consultant to my previous summer employer, RMV systems management. At RMV, I developed an internal software tracking system. I also interacted with several large clients, offering solutions to their software problems and refining my ability to deal with customers in a professional situation.

During my senior year of college, I served as the residential advisor for a coed freshman dorm housing 250 students. Thanks to this experience, I am comfortable assuming a leadership role and ensuring that the goals of a group are met. I believe these skills contribute greatly to my technical qualifications as a systems engineer.

I have enclosed my resume, and I will call your office in two weeks to discuss any openings you might have.

Sincerely,

Hal Simms

Chapter 4
Creative Job Finding Methods

FINDING POTENTIAL EMPLOYERS WHEN OPPORTUNITY DOESN'T KNOCK...
I Guess That On-Campus Interview Thing Was A Pretty Good Deal

"A wise man will make more opportunities than he finds."
—Sir Francis Bacon

Looking for a job is a lot like climbing a ladder. When you graduate, you are down there on the bottom rung with the rest of your class and the rest of the classes across the country. With each job hunting task you tackle, and conquer, you're climbing up one more rung on the ladder. This puts you ahead of those job hunters who don't develop a good resume or don't worry about using a cover letter.

At first, it's a scary thought, but the great thing is that this process can work to your advantage. By the time you get to the critical step in the ladder of finding potential employers, you're probably about to jump ahead of half of the other job hunters out there.

It's at this point, finding potential employers, that many job seekers our age drop out of the competition, but they don't even know it. Maybe they drop out by waiting around for jobs to come to them. Maybe they drop out by looking for jobs through the most obvious methods, like on-campus interviews or ads in the paper, but they don't use the more creative, and successful, methods for finding jobs which we'll discuss in this chapter.

Whatever the problem, this process of elimination puts you one step ahead. If you follow a few simple rules, you can look for jobs in ways in which some of your classmates never dreamed. And the more jobs you know about, the greater your chances of finding the job that is right for you.

In this chapter, we'll look at all of the ways you can find a job, not just at the most obvious ones. We'll explore the benefits and drawbacks of each method and the advantages of looking for a job through several different avenues.

If you take a creative, far-flung approach to job hunting, your job search will be more exciting and more interesting. It will probably be a lot shorter too. At the end of this chapter, you can determine what mix of job hunting methods you'll use, and set some concrete goals for finding employers.

There are four primary methods of job hunting. The first involves responding to ads, the second sending out mass mailings, the third using job banks and the fourth networking.

Networking can sound obnoxious and agonizing. Luckily, networking doesn't mean anything more than meeting people in the field in which you're interested. It consists of telling these people that you want a job and asking if they have any advice. It's straightforward, easy and even somewhat fun.

Networking is such a big part of job hunting that it overlaps with all of the job hunting methods we're going to discuss in this chapter. Since there's so much to cover with networking, we'll wait until Chapter 5 to discuss it fully. If you have the attitude I used to have towards networking, you probably wish we wouldn't discuss it at all. Once you've found a great job through networking, though, it will all be worth it.

"My Job Search Is Classified"

The first major way to find a job is through the classified ads (which are also called the want ads). The classifieds are a convenient, easy-to-use source. To be honest, I had never looked at the classifieds in my life until I looked for a job, and I couldn't have told you what they were, where they were or what they were used for.

Classifieds are the part of the newspaper where employers pay to list jobs they have available. Depending upon the size of the city you live in, the classifieds are a separate section of the paper, like the business section, the sports section, etc. Of course, if you succumb to the mental state of mind known as "Job Hunter's Syndrome," you will begin to think that the classifieds are the newspaper, and all that other stuff in there is just filler.

There are many reasons to use the classified ads in your job search. The first is because you know there is a job available. The second is because it is easy. Of course, we've all had our bad experiences with something someone else says is easy. If your's was when your roommate's brilliant girlfriend persuaded you to take chemistry for a grade rather than pass/fail because chemistry was so easy, I can understand why you're a little nervous.

The listings in the classifieds are alphabetical by job category. Under each category, you will find a brief paragraph describing an individual job. It will often include the salary, and it will give either the employer's address or a post office box number to which you can send in your resume and cover letter.

Classifieds often don't give the companies' names because some companies prefer to remain anonymous when they look for employees. You don't need to worry, however. Companies which only put in a post office box are still usually legitimate job prospects. Often, even the largest and best-known companies in the field will opt for an anonymous ad.

The classifieds are full of strange abbreviations, and it takes a little while to figure each one out. For example, instead of saying that a job pays $20,000 a year, it will just say $20K. The classifieds are also full of strange job categories, such as forestry associate and punch out operator.

I assume that forestry associates help out around the forest with Smokey the Bear, and I have no idea what punch out operators do. When I looked for my first job, after seeing listing after listing for punch out operator, I began to think I was in the wrong career field. Once I could get my attention away from that mysterious category, however, I usually found quite a few potential jobs in the classifieds—and you can too.

I was looking for a career that involved writing, so I looked under advertising, editing, journalism, public affairs, public relations, reporting, and writing. On a bad day, I probably looked under party planner, movie star, ballerina, and personal shopper.

I give you all these listings to illustrate how many different places you can look in the classifieds to find basically the same type of job. You can probably find five or six categories in the classifieds that apply to your career field, and some of them may be in categories about which you would never have thought. But those darn classifieds. They always seem to leave out the important categories, like European Traveler and King of the World.

Don't be afraid to look far and wide under job descriptions you've never considered. It never hurts to interview for a lot of different jobs that all require the same skills. In starting your job hunt with a broad perspective, you can eliminate jobs that don't appeal to you, and you never know what you may turn up that will be of interest.

The best way to use the classifieds is to take some time going through them to familiarize yourself with all of the different headings and types of jobs listed. Once you have some ideas of the categories that apply to you, you should look every day, whether it's a part of your daily job hunting routine or something you do while you're hanging around your apartment with your roommates.

The Sunday paper will yield the greatest number of job possibilities, because the classified section is much bigger on Sundays. In some cities, Thursdays are also big days for classified listings. Surprisingly, you will sometimes find a wonderful job listed once or twice during the week, but not at all during the huge stack of listings on Sunday. For this reason, you should check every day.

You should also consider checking the part-time listings. As we discussed earlier, you never know where a part-time job might lead. As you look for a full-time job, it will encourage you if you're working at least part-time in your career field.

Understanding The Want Ads

Perhaps the biggest trick to using the classifieds is figuring out what a want ad really says. Most ads try to say it all in about twenty words. Usually, fifteen of these words are so abbreviated that it looks like you're learning some kind of new alphabet that doesn't use vowels. This makes it hard to figure out what an employer wants.

Luckily, after you've used the classifieds for a week or so, it becomes easier to tell the amazing opportunities from the dismal dead-ends. Here are a couple of things to keep in mind as you use the classifieds.

First, don't avoid a great job because of an intimidating ad. Employers' want ads are the equivalent of the picture you hold in your mind of the dream job. They call for the ideal candidate. Employers may realize that there's not anyone who meets all of their criteria, and they may be including a wide range of skills so they can find the best person available.

Even if you haven't done exactly what an ad calls for, you may be the type of person for which they are looking. Unless a job requires a skill that is way beyond you, such as a graduate degree or fluency in a language you don't speak, add a concise and convincing paragraph to your cover letter and send in your resume.

This is a key point. I noticed when I was using the classifieds that I could never predict which employers would call me back when I sent in my resume. I would see ads that I thought practically described my resume word for word, yet I would not hear from the company. Other jobs looked like a real stretch, and I would almost feel stupid for sending in my resume because I was so under-qualified. It turned out that those were some of the jobs about which I received calls.

The second part of reading between the lines of the classified ads involves looking for phrases that indicate that the employer wants little more than a glorified secretary. If an ad calls for "good typing skills," "light secretarial work" or an "administrative assistant," this may not be the best opportunity for you. It could be that this job would lead to more substantive work, but you should maintain a healthy skepticism for jobs that wouldn't fully utilize your skills.

One issue which can pose problems for recent college grads is determining the worth of a position as an administrative assistant. In some fields, such as advertising, public relations and journalism, this can be a good place for a recent college graduate to start.

For example, as an administrative assistant at a public relations firm, you might set up and attend client meetings, write smaller pieces, such as client bios or follow-up letters, and generally learn more about the field. In this case, you are gradually acquiring the specific job skills you need to move up to the next level, and you are assumed to be working towards an eventual promotion.

In some fields, however, beginning your career as an administrative assistant could be a mistake. While you may be given vague promises about the potential for advancement, you are really serving as a secretary. As an ambitious college graduate, you should probably avoid those administrative assistant positions which never require anything more than data entry and other clerical chores. You may not find any opportunity for advancement with that company, and you are unlikely to learn anything substantive to take to your next employer.

As you try to decide if a position as an administrative assistant would be right for you, you can best make that decision by listening closely in an interview—and by asking a few discerning questions. We'll talk about this later on in the chapter on interviewing. For now, use your best judgment. If a job sounds great, go ahead and respond with your resume and a cover letter, no matter what the title.

You've probably already heard a lot about having to pay your dues and work your way up, but you'll be doing yourself a big favor if you try to start out at the highest level that is reasonable for a recent college graduate.

There is nothing more frustrating than ending up in a stressful and demanding job in which you don't really do anything more than make the boss' coffee and type for fifteen different people all day. Especially if other recent college graduates with your same level of experience came in one step higher than you because they didn't fall for the pay-your-dues routine. We'll get into this more in the assertiveness chapter. You should view yourself as an intelligent person who deserves to get the best job for which you are qualified.

As you become a savvy user of the classifieds, you'll start to see a few jobs that frequently reappear in the classifieds. Be wary about responding to these ads. There must be some reason the company either can't find someone or can't hold on to them once they hire them. You just don't want to find out why first-hand.

As you can see, the more carefully you evaluate an ad before responding, the better your chances of finding a job you'll love. But no matter how many good jobs you find through the classifieds, if you rely on the newspaper alone, you'll miss out on a lot of other opportunities. The classifieds are a readily available and easy-to-use source for jobs, but they don't tell you about all the great jobs.

"Often, it's who you know that helps you get a job," comments career counselor Sherrie Pavol Bereda of Career Concepts. "Many jobs aren't advertised, or if they are, they are filled before the ad is ever published."

This is because someone already working at the company decides to try for the job or someone at the company tells a friend of a friend about the job and they get it. If you want to be one of those people on the inside track who finds out about jobs before they're advertised, you should branch out into other methods of job hunting.

"Of Course This Isn't A Form Letter"

Mass mailings are a good way to supplement your use of the classifieds. Sending a mass mailing means sending out what is basically a form letter to a list of employers, whether that means 25 companies, 50 companies or 200. You can do a mass mailing without a lot of effort if you have a well-written cover letter which appears to be fairly personalized.

There are a lot of benefits to mass mailings. You can run across jobs that aren't being advertised yet or of which you were unaware. You can explore a different aspect of your career field, and you may even uncover jobs you might never have considered before. You can meet a lot of people, or network, which we'll discuss later. Just try to prevent your letter from sounding like one of those rambling, impersonal Christmas letters that people send to 800 of their closest friends.

To send out a mass mailing, you need a list of companies with jobs similar to the one you want. This is probably the part of the process that takes the most work.

Creating Your List

Find a good library in your city, whether it is the main library, a suburban branch, or a business library affiliated with a college or university. Once you've located a library, head for the reference section to find books which contain lists of potential employers.

You will be amazed at how many different lists of companies there are. There are lists of the biggest companies in your area, the fastest growing, the largest in any one industry or, best of all, every single company in a certain field. You can find lists that split up the country geographically so you can emerge with the names of companies in your own area.

For example, National Trade and Professional Associations of the U.S. (Columbia Books, Inc.) and the Encyclopedia of Associations (Cole Research) are a good place to start. Depending upon the field in which you're interested, you can find a wealth of reference materials to help you pinpoint potential employers. If you need assistance in locating the right sources in your library, be sure to talk to the reference librarian. Explain that you're conducting a job search, and ask for any ideas the librarian might have.

In looking for a writing job, I found, and used, lists of advertising agencies, public relations firms, speech-writing groups, newspapers, publishers, newsletters and more. There are lists of law firms, engineering firms, government agencies, large corporations, etc.

The different types of lists go on and on, and if you're willing to spend a few hours in the library and do some photocopying, you can walk out with the names of hundreds of potential employers, especially if you live in a big city.

In addition to straight lists, there are surveys. Where I live, one of the major newspapers publishes a yearly survey of the 25 largest or best (or whatever category they've created) law firms, engineering firms, etc. in the metropolitan area. This list is a tremendous resource for job hunters. It gives the company name, address, phone, product or service, years in business and a very brief history. A lot of other publications publish similar lists, whether it's a Fortune 500 magazine or a local publication's listing of area employers.

If you find a specific back issue of a newspaper or magazine with all of this information, you can often order it directly from the publisher. This will save you both the time and expense of photocopying long lists at the library.

After you've developed your lists, look over them to see which companies might employ someone with your talents. Try to be creative. For example, if you've got a degree in accounting, you could work for virtually any kind of company.

The first places you might think of working are the larger or better known accounting firms, but you could also work for a local business or a non-profit organization. Developing good lists for your mass mailing can take thought, but can broaden your possibilities considerably.

Surprisingly, the phone book can be another good source of companies to add to your list. It can also help you think of places to send your resume that you might not have considered before.

Career counselor Susan Schubert of Schubert & Associates suggests you flip through the yellow pages with a set of key words in mind. For example, if you know you'd like to work in health care, but the only places you've considered are doctors' offices and hospitals, you could develop a more complete list by going through the phone book.

Your list might end up including insurance companies, health maintenance organizations, nursing homes, social services agencies, AM-PM clinics, etc. Developing a list of key words is effective regardless of your major or career interests. Schubert advises that you include any employment category that sounds like it might match up with your skills. You can always eliminate one of your key words if you don't like the jobs that fall under that heading.

"Before job hunting candidates send out resumes, it's

important that they identify what they can do," explains Schubert. "Use the phone book or use reference books and other publications to find career fields and job titles."

"Did You Say Mass Mailing Or Mass Confusion?"

Whether you're sending out mass mailings, responding to ads, or both, General Motors' personnel manager James Sturtz stresses the importance of conducting your job hunt in an organized way. This will keep you from getting confused and allow you to cover the field more completely.

"Focus on companies that have opportunities for you rather than taking a shotgun approach," advises Sturtz. This means targeting two or three specific job categories, whether from the phone book or from lists you've created, and devoting your time and attention to these positions. Some recent grads aimlessly send one letter to an insurance agency and another to a bank and feel like they've exhausted their opportunities.

Recruiter John Stone from Chrysler suggests that if you use mass mailings, you select those companies in which you're most interested. While this is easier said than done, you might be able to figure out which companies are best suited to your interests by asking a former professor or employer.

Or you could consult one of your mass mailing lists and see which are the biggest or the fastest growing or the most civic minded or whatever it is that is most important to you. Concentrate your letter writing and follow-up on the jobs that seem to best match up with your skills.

"Pick out the companies you are genuinely interested in and tailor your cover letter," says Stone. "Have a first tier and a second tier."

There is one drawback to conducting mass mailings, and that is that you have no idea if there is a position available at the organization you're contacting. And since larger companies may not be as willing to interview you if they don't have a position available, mass mailings may be more effective for smaller companies.

"We do hire students who send us unsolicited resumes, but not as often as we hire students through on-campus interviews," Stone comments.

For smaller companies, however, mass mailings can open a lot of doors. Whether or not your job search lends itself well to mass mailings is something you can decide depending upon your own circumstances and the type of job for which you're looking. If you have the time, though, it never hurts to send out a resume, and you can end up with a lot more than you ever would have thought possible.

As Ford's college recruiter Darrell Washington expresses it, "You don't want to not do something, like send out a resume, that could enhance your opportunities."

Using Job Banks

Responding to the classifieds and sending out mass mailings are the two primary ways to put your name in front of potential employers, but there are other methods, such as using job banks.

Job banks are listings of jobs available in certain fields. I know of several job banks which list positions in journalism, advertising, public relations and government affairs. I'm sure there are countless others in practically every career field you can imagine.

You can find these job banks through professional associations or through contacts you've met while networking. We'll discuss both of these possibilities in the next chapter.

Job banks vary widely and are as good as the individual organization which runs them. Most job banks require membership in the group. Membership dues for professional associations range from $50 to $125 per year. Often, there are various tiers of membership, such as student member, associate member, full member, etc. Recent college graduates frequently can join as associate members and pay a slightly reduced membership fee.

Most job banks work in a straightforward manner. Usually, you call a phone number and listen to a tape recorded description of each job, the qualifications the employer is seeking and the salary. The recorded listing gives all of the information except for the name of the employer.

You then call the person in charge of the job bank, give your name, and ask for more information, such as the employer's name and address. The rest is up to you. If you're interested in the job, you send your resume and cover letter.

To participate in job banks that rely on written listings, you can put yourself on the organization's mailing list and receive job bank updates through the mail. If possible, you can save time by going to the organization and picking up the updated listings every week or month.

Clearly, the more current the job bank listings, the more useful they will be to you. When evaluating a job bank, ask yourself these questions: How many new listings appear each time the job bank is updated? How often is the job bank updated? Where else are these jobs publicized? How often do employers fill the jobs with people using the job bank?

Some organizations require an additional fee for use of the job bank. I would hesitate to pay extra for a job bank, because, like the classifieds, there is no guarantee you can find a job.

You could consider using a job bank that charges a fee if the fee is nominal or if there is an opportunity for you to try the job bank first without paying for it. It also might help if you could get a refund if you give the job bank a trial run and you're not satisfied.

The benefits of job banks are the same as those of classified ads, in that you know there are specific job openings and you simply have to regularly consult one source, the job bank, for new information on potential employers.

The drawbacks of a job bank lie in how good the job bank is that you are using. If the job bank is rarely updated, or if it doesn't advertise good jobs, it probably won't be too helpful. However, if you've found a good job bank, it can provide you with all kinds of opportunities.

Here is a partial listing of job banks I found in my local library.

- If you're interested in careers in the arts, there is "ArtSEARCH, The National Employment Service Bulletin for the Arts." It is published by Theatre Communications Group, Inc. in New York City.
- If you're interested in non-profit organizations, check out "Community Jobs," published by James Clark in Boston, Massachusetts. If you'd like to learn more about non-profits dedicated to protecting the environment, check out "Earth Work," a monthly listing published by the Student Conservation Association in Charleston, New Hampshire. There is also a job bank publication entitled "1991 Helping Out In The Outdoors," which gives information about internships on public lands. This job bank lead sheet is published by the American Hiking Society in Washington, D.C.
- If you'd like to enter a career in library science, look in

"Career Leads," published by the American Libraries Association in Chicago, Illinois.

- A larger and more general job bank which includes classifieds from all over the country in practically every field is the "National Ad Search." This weekly publication is published out of Milwaukee, Wisconsin.

Again, the best way for you to get started is to go to your library and ask the reference librarian to steer you in the right direction. As you can see from this abbreviated list, there are job banks for all interests. As you explore all of your options, try to identify those job banks which would be helpful to you and use them on a regular basis.

Insuring The Accuracy Of Your List

Once you've found prospective jobs, whether through the classifieds, through lists at the library or through a job bank, your next step is to confirm the name and address of every employer on your list.

Yes, this is another one of those ways you have to adapt to real life after you graduate. Unlike on-campus mail, you actually have to address your mail accurately. And you'll probably have to be more careful with the addresses on your personal correspondence too, since mailing little scraps of paper addressed only to "Wild Man" won't cut it with the U.S. Postal Service.

Calling to confirm the addresses of potential employers may sound like a lot of work, but it can help you climb up one more rung on the ladder. No matter how up-to-date any list is, there are going to be companies that have gone out of business, moved, merged with another company or simply changed names. First impressions count, and if your letter is delivered to the company under the wrong name, you may have wasted an opportunity for an interview. Of course, if it isn't delivered at all, you can write that one off.

For all of the other job hunters who went as far as developing a list for a mass mailing, very few will take the time to get the name of a specific person at the company or to confirm the mailing address. This is good for you because it's one more way to eliminate some of the competition for what may become your job.

Calling each employer is most critical when you're using a list that you've developed. If you are responding to an ad in the paper or a job listed in a job bank, you may have all of the information you need without making any calls.

As you confirm the address of each company on your list, you can also get the name of the person to whom you should send your resume. In general, you should send your resume to the head of the division for which you're interested in working.

There are several reasons for starting at the top when you send out letters seeking employment. Senior level people are more likely to speak to you than the human resources office is, especially if the company doesn't have a job available at the time you inquire.

In addition, the president of the company or the head of the department may view speaking to you as more of a professional courtesy. She might want to help out someone younger who is entering her field.

When I was looking for my first job, I was encouraged by the fact that I ran across a lot of people who were willing to speak to me, give me advice or give me the name of someone else to call. I often found these people by directing my resume and cover letter to someone near the top of the company's hierarchy.

Some job applicants like to send a copy of the letter to

human resources in order to cover all of their bases. This is a good idea, and it also lets you play by the rules of the corporate hiring process. By notifying the human resources or personnel office that you've written the president or vice-president of the company (or of the division in which you're interested), you're indicating that you're not trying to evade their formal system for bringing in new people.

Indicate that you're sending two copies by typing cc: followed by the name of the person to whom you're sending the extra letter. For example, if you're writing Brian Thompson in marketing and Jane Rogers in personnel, address your letter to Brian Thompson and put cc: Jane Rogers at the bottom of the page after your name.

Using The Phone To Your Advantage

While it's easy to make the call to confirm a name and address, it helps if you have a general idea of what to expect when you call. It can be intimidating to call the company for which you hope to work, but after you've made a few calls, you can develop a system that works for you.

You can start the call by saying that you want to confirm the address and by reading off what you have. Some lists give a president's name so you can also confirm the spelling of his or her name at this time.

If no names are listed, ask for the name of the company president or the director of the department in which you're interested. At this point, a receptionist will often ask either who is calling or why you're calling.

State your name and don't worry about it. It is unlikely the receptionist will record your name or mention your call to someone higher up in the company. If she does, it simply looks like you'd like to work there.

If she asks why you're calling, explain. Tell the receptionist that you plan to send in your resume, and you want to make sure you have the correct information. Explain that you want to get the name of a specific person at the company so your resume won't get lost.

It's easy to get paranoid when you're job hunting, especially when you've just graduated, and you feel like one wrong step will ruin everything. Keep in mind, though, that when you're looking for a job, your main objective is to present yourself well. If you have to make a few phone calls and ask a few questions in order to do that, that's fine.

In addition, when you call to get the necessary information, some receptionists will tell you that there aren't any jobs available. Don't let that stop you. You're interested in sending in your resume whether or not a job is currently available. There could be jobs coming up down the road that the receptionist doesn't know about. Or the president's next door neighbor may own a similar company and may be looking for new people. The possibilities go on and on, and you can't let negative words from a few people deter you in your job search.

Now that you're aware of the many sources of potential jobs—and of the importance of sending your resume to the right person—you can decide which mix of job hunting methods you would like to use. After you've selected your methods and sent out some letters, you're ready to follow up with the employers you've contacted.

Fabulous Follow Up

You may have thought you'd made all of the phone calls you needed to make when you confirmed the names and addresses of employers, but that was just the beginning. Now is the time to distinguish yourself from other applicants by following up on your letter and resume.

Follow-up calls are one of the most critical parts of a job search. You can send out literally hundreds of resumes and cover letters, but you are unlikely to find a job unless you take the initiative and contact employers to request an interview.

Follow-up calls actually serve several purposes. First, by making a follow-up call, you can verify that the employers received your resume. Second, you can demonstrate that you really want the job. Third, if you can impress potential employers through a brief phone conversation, you will be able to interview even if there's not a job available. This way, you've made a valuable contact, and when a job does become available, you could be first in line.

How you choose to follow up with employers depends upon the circumstances under which you send in your resume. If you sent in your resume in response to a classified ad or a job bank listing, you should give the employers some time to look over all of the resumes that are sent in. The employers are probably swamped with resumes, and you want to make yourself stand out for your attention to detail, not for your pushy approach.

A good rule of thumb is to wait to call employers until approximately one week after you've sent your resume. After that time, you can call employers and ask to speak to the person in charge of hiring. If you know the person's name, simply ask for him or her.

The issue of what to call an employer used to disturb me as much as finding the perfect interview suit. If you call and ask for Mr. Jones, it immediately sounds like you are young and perhaps not worthy of speaking to Mr. Jones. Worse yet, it might sound like you're trying to sell him something. (Of course, you are, in a sense, but the receptionist doesn't need to know that.) If you call and ask for Bob Jones, it can make you feel like you're pretending to be on a first name basis with the man.

I found it most effective to call and ask for Bob Jones, but then, of course, to address him as Mr. Jones once he was on the line. It doesn't matter if he answers the phone and hears you ask for Bob Jones, because once you begin speaking to him, you'll call him Mr. Jones.

It's amazing how earth-shattering each of these fine points of etiquette becomes in your mind once you start job hunting. But your initial phone call goes a long way in creating a first impression on potential employers.

According to John Stewart of The Austin Company, poor phone manners are often the first way many job seekers blow their chances for an interview.

"I don't like having to dig information out of someone over the phone," explains Stewart. "Some applicants make the worst presentation over the phone. They call up and say 'I'm Ed Smith, and I'm looking for a job.'"

In Stewart's opinion, job seekers would make a better impression if they volunteered information more freely. While Stewart and other employers don't want a sales pitch over the phone, they'd like to hear what your background is, such as your major or the name of your college, and they'd like a brief statement as to why you'd be good for the job.

It might be as simple as saying, "I'm interested in the job you advertised, and I think my experience with (fill in the blank) in college would make me a good applicant."

Use the same judgment in your follow-up that you used in writing your resume. You don't want to go overboard, calling people up and describing yourself in glowing terms, but you shouldn't make employers drag all of the relevant information out of you.

It helps if you deal with employers in the same way you would deal with professors you wanted to favorably impress. If you had to go to your professor's office to talk about something, you wouldn't discuss your brilliance and the number of hours you study, but you wouldn't come in and stand there mutely either. The best approach with employers is to be natural and to be willing to talk about yourself and your qualifications.

Once you've made a few calls, you shouldn't have any problems presenting yourself well to employers. It just takes a little practice and advance planning. If you keep in mind that conversations require effort on both sides, you can present yourself as a well-organized and articulate candidate.

If you make a follow-up phone call and you're able to reach the person who received your resume, ask if you will be able to come in for an interview. Express your interest in working for the company and briefly highlight one or two of your strong points from your resume.

For example, you could say, "This is Tim Smith, and I'm calling to follow-up on the resume I sent you one week ago. As you may recall, I graduated in the top fourth of my class with a degree in engineering, and I worked for one of my professors last summer on a research project involving the use of synthetic materials on the space shuttle."

After the employer indicates that she remembers you, or even if she doesn't remember you, ask if you can come in for an interview. You could say, "I'm interested in coming in for an interview, and I wondered if we could set up a time at your convenience." If she says she is still reviewing resumes, ask when would be a good time to call back. You can close the conversation by saying, "I will call your office in two weeks as you have suggested, and I look forward to speaking to you then."

If you aren't able to get through to the person who has your resume, give it another few days and call once more. When you call, ask to speak to the person who has your resume. Tell the receptionist that you're calling to inquire about the status of your resume.

This phone call serves a practical purpose. If you're no longer being considered, you will find that out, and you will not waste any more time focusing on that job. If you are still being considered, you're bringing your name to the employer's attention, and that little nudge could be all it takes to persuade him to bring you in for an interview.

"It's the squeaky wheel that gets the grease, and often, persistence can win you a job," says Pavol Bereda. "If an employer says they'll know who they're going to interview in one week, call them in a week."

According to Pavol Bereda, many companies hold off on making a decision, either on who to interview or who to hire, until they see who has the initiative to call and ask if they're being considered.

If you make your follow-up calls and the person you're trying to reach won't speak to you, ask the receptionist if there is a certain time of day that is a good time to reach the employer. You can often tell by the receptionist's attitude if the person really is hard to reach or if he is not interested in taking your call.

Of course, if it is a big company, the receptionist may not know when is the best time to call. A good rule of thumb is to stop calling if you place three or four calls over a week or two and never get any kind of response.

Keeping Accurate Records

As you look for a job, you will probably send out close to a hundred letters and make twice as many phone calls. If you keep track of who you send letters to, who you call and what you discuss in each phone call, it will be easier to keep yourself organized.

Now you can start using that filing system we discussed in Chapter 1. There isn't a right way or a wrong way to keep track of your job hunt, as long as what you're doing works for you. Sometimes, though, it's easier to develop your own system if you have some general guidelines to follow.

Consider starting your filing system with four files. The first is for letters you've sent out but haven't followed up on yet, the second for letters on which you need to take some action, the third for letters that are pending and the fourth for rejections.

In the first file, you can keep letters that you've sent out and haven't had time to pursue. This is handy when employers start to call you as well. You can turn to your first file and pull out a copy of the letter you sent. In doing this, you can also see the mass mailing list on which the employer's name falls or the classified ad or whatever it was that prompted you to send in your resume.

In the second file, you can keep letters that require some action on your part, whether it is an initial follow-up phone call, an interview, or, once you start interviewing, a thank you note.

In the third file, you can keep letters from companies from which you haven't heard anything. This will probably end up being your largest file as you continue sending out letters. Never throw away any correspondence from a potential employer, even if the person to whom you sent your resume won't take your calls and it's been two months since you sent your letter in.

Job hunting can be an unusual process. You may not hear anything from specific companies for a long time, and it might simply mean they're busy and they've put off hiring for a little while. They may then call you when you least expect it, so unless you have some reason to believe a company has rejected you without telling you, keep your pending file full.

You can use the fourth file for your rejection letters. It makes sense to save a rejection letter because you can write notes about the company on their letter. For example, you may interview for a job and get rejected. If you thought the job looked boring and you wouldn't want to work there, write that down. You may get called in again by that company at some point in the future, and it can help you make decisions about whether or not you want to try for another position there.

Or, you may interview and get rejected by a company, but decide that you'd eventually like to work there. Write down all of your perceptions of the interview and the company, and file the rejection letter away for future reference.

File all of your letters in chronological order, no matter which of the four categories they're in. It's easiest if you file them with the most recent letters on top and the oldest letters on the bottom.

Now that you're familiar with a basic filing system, you can figure out how to keep track of your job hunt. If you send a form letter to 50 banks, copy one copy before you send it. You can then keep only one copy of the letter and a list with the names of the 50 banks to which you sent your letter.

If you send one letter to 50 banks and a slightly modified letter to 25 accounting firms, keep a copy of both letters and keep two lists of names. The first list will be of the 50 banks which received letter A and the second of the 25 accounting firms which received letter B. And if you ever work for the

Publisher's Clearinghouse Sweepstakes, these mass mailing skills will put you way ahead of the game.

As you start calling all of the banks on your list, keep track of who you speak to at each bank. Write down the date that you called them (or that they called you). Write down what they say, whether it's that they've filled the job with someone else, they're still thinking about it or they'd like you to call back in three weeks.

If an employer tells you to call them back in three weeks, write that down in your calendar. It works best if you write down the employer's name and phone number on your calendar page. After three weeks go by, you can pick up the phone and make the two or three calls you need to make that day, without going through your files.

However, it can be helpful to look over your form letter briefly before you call someone back. Reviewing your files will help you remember which collegiate experience you linked to the job or which academic project you mentioned in touting yourself as the most qualified candidate.

If you used a classified ad, staple it to the form letter that you sent. This way, you have all the information at a glance, such as the salary and other details of the job. It's best to know these things before you get on the phone with a potential employer. Keeping this information in one place will greatly speed your follow-up phone calls.

You should also include in your records any phone calls you make that aren't returned. Say you call ABC Manufacturing on June 8, 9, and 12th, and no one calls you back. If you call a lot of other companies during those days, you might not remember that you've placed several calls to ABC which haven't been returned. Or you may not have made the last two calls at all, thinking you'd already tried them and they'd said no.

Therefore, put a note on your list next to ABC Manufacturing. It can be as simple as something like: "6/8, 6/9, 6/12: left message." You might speak to ABC Manufacturing in June, and they'll tell you to call back in July. When you call back in July, they may say there is a hiring freeze, but recommend you call back in early September.

Record this information in your calendar so you'll remember to call back in September if you're still looking for a job. Write down the information about the hiring freeze so when you do call in September, you'll know what's going on with the company. It may sound like there's no point in calling employers a few months down the road if they've already said they don't have any positions available, but you never know what may turn up.

As you have seen, there are several different ways to find potential employers. And once you start sending out letters, your job hunt will begin to get exciting, and believe it or not, even kind of fun. Here are a few ideas to help you move into this phase of finding potential employers.

Making Opportunities Happen

1. Start finding potential employers through the classifieds. Begin looking for jobs today. If you're looking long distance, check out the section below.

2. Make a list of key words and look in the phone book under these different headings. Every day, try to find a new category under which you can find jobs you'd be interested in. Do this until you've got about five or six categories.

3. Begin developing a mass mailing list. As valuable as these lists are, they can take a little more time to put together, so don't become discouraged if this step takes you a while or if you need to put it aside while you respond to the classifieds. Just don't put it off for good!

4. Check out your key word categories at the library, and copy relevant directories. You might want to make your first mass mailing a small one, with 25 companies or so. Try to call five or six of the companies on the list to confirm their addresses each day. This way, you should have a completely accurate list within a week.

5. Find out about job banks or employment hot-lines in your area. If you know of some, spend this week becoming a part of the system. Begin calling the job bank or picking up the listings, and add those opportunities to your employment list. If you have no idea where to find a job bank, hold off on this until you've read the networking chapter.

6. Set up a schedule for beginning your follow-up phone calls, say, two weeks from the time you send out your first resume. After two weeks, call four or five employers to ask about the status of your resume.

7. Take yourself out and reward yourself for making so much progress with your job hunt!

Looking Long Distance

As you put together your game plan for finding potential employers, you'll want to decide exactly where you will look for a job. Will it be in your home town? In your college town, if the two differ? In some great city in which you've always wanted to live? Anywhere you can find a good job?

It could be one of these places or it could be all of them. It's not uncommon for recent graduates to find their job search encompassing several different cities at once.

The long distance job search can pose some unique challenges, but if you utilize the methods outlined in this book, you'll find you can be successful, whether you're looking for jobs that are nearby or far away.

Sarah Hart

"This Couldn't Be Worse Than A Long Distance Relationship"

There are two parts to a long distance job search. The first part involves actually looking in a city which you may never have seen before.

Just as your life has several different components which aren't related to work, your decision as to the city which is best for you will probably include personal factors. You can, however, make a decision that suits both your personal and career needs by carefully assessing your chosen career field.

Are you interested in a career which would flourish in a particular geographic location? For example, recent graduates interested in working their way up in book publishing would want to look closely at Manhattan, as would someone who hopes to someday become a stock broker on Wall Street. Recent graduates interested in the entertainment field, on the other hand, would want to consider Hollywood.

Aspiring television or newspaper reporters might need to get their start in smaller towns while those interested in the restaurant or hotel service industries would probably focus on larger towns. Recent graduates with engineering degrees often find themselves working at plant sites in rural, out-of-the-way areas. If your career would benefit, or, as is the case for many recently graduated engineers, require that you move to a particular city or state, you should probably make that move.

In past years, recent graduates and others seeking employment have flocked to areas of the country experiencing an economic boom. At the time of this writing, it seems that Washington and Oregon come the closest to fitting that description. When I graduated, California and the Northeast were prospering, and in the early '80s, Texas and the Southwest were getting good reviews.

Some career fields, on the other hand, lend themselves to depressed markets, as is the case with bank examiners or work out specialists who take over failing companies. If your goal is to prevent or turn around a bad situation, you might need to seek out the more economically troubled parts of the country to make your big break.

There is some wisdom in moving to a market which appears to have more opportunity than the one in which you are currently located. As you think about basing your choice of cities on the prevailing economic situation, however, you should also take into account the things that make you happy outside of your work life, such as your hobbies and your general life-style.

As you strive to determine which type of city would best suit you, you can consult a variety of books at your local library which rank the "livability" of almost every city in the country. One good example is the Places Rated Almanac. It ranks metropolitan areas by cost of living, job outlook, crime, health, transportation, education, the arts, recreation, the climate and more.

You should also think about the connections you already have or the personal needs you would like to fulfill as you select your future home town. Do you have friends and family in a certain city? Do you love skiing and the outdoors and need somewhere you can get away from it all? Are you an urban person who feels stifled without museums and night-life?

While you are the only one who can decide which city is best for you, especially regarding your personal life, you can use this book to launch a successful long-distance career search after you've selected the city or cities in which you're interested.

A Job Search Is A Job Search Is A...

First, follow all of the steps outlined in this chapter just as you would for a local job search. Purchase a subscription to the major newspapers for the cities in which you're interested.

If this sounds too expensive or difficult for you, you could skip the subscription and drop by the library each day to check out the classified ads in the newspapers for the cities in which you're interested.

The key words here are "each day." While it takes a little research to learn about jobs in distant cities, you will see results if you make a commitment to looking extensively in every city in which you're interested.

Second, even if you're conducting a long-distance job search, you should still engage in the same prospecting and networking process outlined in the next chapter. This means mass mailings are an excellent way for you to locate possible job openings. Just as you would obtain and develop lists of potential employers for the city in which you are currently living, you can also develop lists of employers for cities that are far away.

While you're at the library looking over the newspapers for "your" cities, develop a list of the potential employers located there also. For example, perhaps you're living in New Mexico now, and you'd like to work in the hospitality industry in Atlanta. You know some people there, and you think the job market for restaurant and hotel management will be relatively strong since Atlanta won the bid for the next Summer Olympics.

In this case, you can look up many of the possibilities for employment in Atlanta in the reference books at your library. You might look up the names and addresses of the hotels and restaurants themselves, as well as the trade associations which represent the restaurant and hotel business, the ad agencies and public relations firms who help them generate new business, etc.

Whether you're interested in writing, accounting, project management or translating, you can probably find a position in your chosen field in your chosen city (in this example the hospitality industry in Atlanta) if you will only be creative in putting together the list of potential employers you will contact.

Third, as you'll discover in the chapter on finding potential employers, you should think broadly as you begin your job search, even when some of your ideas sound a little wacky. It never hurts to interview for jobs you never strongly considered, and you might learn more about yourself and your interests.

For this example, you'd obtain the names and addresses of companies located in Atlanta from reference books. You'd either subscribe to the *Atlanta Constitution* or check out the job listings in the library's copy of the paper. You'd also want to make sure you weren't missing out on the want ads in smaller community papers serving the Atlanta area.

Fourth, supplement your knowledge of the communities in which you'd like to live by calling the local Chambers of Commerce there. The Chamber of Commerce offices in many cities have a toll-free 800 number, and the people who work there will be happy to send you information on employment, housing, entertainment, leisure activities and more.

Simply call the Chamber of Commerce for the city in which you are interested, and they will send you this information free of charge. You should also mention that you are job hunting, and ask if they have a list of large and small employers in the area. They may have a more extensive list than you would find in the library, with information about the age of the company, the number of people it employs and the product or service it offers.

A Chamber of Commerce may also be able to steer you to local job banks, such as one provided by the county or by one of the libraries. It can also help you locate the libraries in the area.

Fifth, call the reference librarian at the library you've decided to use in this far away town. Tell her you're conducting a long distance job hunt and you would like any information she could send you. She might send you much of the same information sent by the Chamber of Commerce, but she's likely to know of additional job hunting resources.

These are all "freebies," except for the phone calls, and you can save yourself a lot of time and energy by getting organized before you simply show up in a strange town and start knocking on doors.

"I Guess I Shouldn't Have Scheduled Interviews In San Francisco and Boston On The Same Day!"

There are a few difficulties in engaging in a long distance job hunt, though, and these obstacles will be most apparent when you network and follow-up.

Clearly, if you've sent in your resume long distance, the employer is aware that you are not available locally for interviews and networking meetings. This is not a problem, and does not reflect poorly on you, but it may mean you will have to pay your own expenses when you travel to this far away city for an interview.

In some cases, employers will pay your way, but it all depends upon the size and policies of the company and the demand for someone with your skills. Unfortunately, it seems to be more the exception than the rule to find employers willing to pay for your travel, especially if you're contacting the employer on your own after graduation rather than as part of the on-campus interview cycle.

Employers usually won't pay your way to informational interviews since these interviews are conducted as a courtesy to you. However, you can hold your long distance job hunting costs to a minimum, whether you're going on "real" interviews or on informational interviews, if you will engage in some well-planned scheduling. Careful scheduling will also allow you to maximize your networking contacts.

First, when you conduct your follow-up phone call, express your eagerness to come in for an interview. Explain that you will be in town during a certain week, and try to schedule every meeting during that time. If you make the most of your time visiting each city for interviews, you can accomplish quite a bit on a limited budget.

When you go to this new city, use any networking contacts you can think of, even for your personal life. Call a friend of a friend to ask about the cost and location of apartments. When you look through the classifieds as part of your library research, take that time to look at the real estate ads as well.

Make your interview trips as productive as possible by learning something about each city before you arrive. Perhaps rush hour traffic is extremely bad and you would waste valuable hours if you scheduled appointments in the late afternoon. Perhaps there is some type of apartment locator service in a major shopping mall which would reduce the time you spend learning about the cost and availability of housing.

In general, you should limit your long distance interviewing to three or four cities, unless some great opportunity presents itself to you in a far away city which is not on your list. As you hone and refine your job hunting goals through the entire job hunting process, you may decide a certain city is not for you, whether for personal or professional reasons. If this is the case, strike it from your list and focus your energy on the remaining cities in which you're interested.

As you evaluate whether or not to look long distance, you can make your decision more easily by thinking about your individual life-style, your choice of career fields and the economic realities of the area of the country in which you're looking.

Whether you look locally or long distance, however, if you'll begin in an organized way and keep an open mind, you can find valuable contacts and a wealth of job opportunities.

NETWORKING YOUR WAY TO GREATNESS, EVEN WHEN YOU DON'T KNOW ANYONE ANYWHERE...
No Problem, Doing Lunch Is My Strong Point

"Small opportunities are often the beginnings of great enterprises."
—Demosthenes

Successful networking is the cornerstone of job hunting. As we've already learned, most jobs are filled before they are advertised. Who you know, or who you meet through an assertive, well-organized job hunt, can help you get where you want to go.

I thought networking was for some kind of pushy and

insincere social climber, such as the type of person who uses obnoxious buzz-words like network in daily conversation. Or it was for wealthy and well-connected fraternity presidents who probably didn't even need a job in the first place. Since I wouldn't want to be in the first category, and I'm not in the second category, I didn't consider networking to be an option. Besides, I didn't know anyone in the city to which I was moving.

Fortunately, I was completely wrong in my assessment of networking. (Someday, you may be wrong about something too.) It turned out that networking is easy, interesting, fun, and extremely helpful. Best of all, it's something any recent graduate can do. So get rid of any pre-conceived notions you may have about networking, and get ready to take part in what may be the biggest and most important part of your job hunt.

First, the facts about networking. Networking can lead you to jobs you may never have known existed. For you as a recent college graduate, networking is nothing more than talking to people about their jobs, asking how you can enter the field and obtaining names of people you can talk to about that field. In this way, networking will enable you to learn what it is that people in your chosen career really do.

It can give you a more realistic picture of what it means to have the career you're seeking, and it may allow you to redirect your job hunting focus if you decide you're not looking for the job that will really make you happy.

Networking can help you not only as you look for your first job, but it can also help you plant seeds for your future. If you keep up with the people who help you when you first graduate, you can continue to benefit from knowing them as you move forward in your chosen career field. Through networking, you can develop valuable professional relationships and possibly a few personal friendships as well.

The first step of networking is best described by a term we'll call "prospecting." Prospecting is a way to find out about the potential sources of networking contacts and, of course, jobs. Prospecting involves sending your resume to a wide range of companies without knowing if any jobs are actually available. If there are jobs available, you have found additional "prospects" for interviewing and for eventual employment, hence the name "prospecting."

Prospecting is the premise behind the mass mailing approach, and we will discuss it later in this chapter.

When you network, the step that comes after prospecting, you should keep in mind that you have several goals. One is to make a favorable impression on the person you're meeting in case they learn of a job opening for which you're qualified. The other is to walk away from your meeting with one name or one suggestion, whether it is the name of one of their colleagues or some kind of advice about your resume. It would be nice to walk away with the keys to their car or an invitation to their beach house, but unfortunately, networking doesn't seem to get quite that rewarding!

The best thing you can hope to gain from networking is a firm job offer, and that's always possible. However, you have to take a more broad view of the job hunt when you network, and realize that each name you gather or each piece of advice you pick up is one more small gain in your search.

Networking yields a lot of advantages, but it might not be anything as dramatic and final as a job offer, at least not at the very first. It's a complex and subtle process, and it requires a little bit of patience!

There are four major ways to prospect and network:
- talking to professors, former employers, family and friends to get the names of people to contact

- sending out mass mailings
- joining any type of alumni group available to you
- attending job hunter's workshops offered in your community.

Just as you used a mix of job hunting methods when you looked for potential employers, you should use a mix of networking methods to insure the greatest success.

You Have Contacts—Really!

Talking to professors, former employers, friends and family members is probably the most obvious method of networking. If you know a professor well enough to ask for help finding a job, by all means, do it. You may be able to ask professors if they know of anyone working in your field.

"If you're a recent college graduate and you want to begin networking, professors are often the best place to start," says career counselor Dr. Ray Harrison of Manchester. "They may have connections outside with companies for which they do consulting work, and they might be able to provide you with an introduction."

It's easier to ask professors and other networking contacts to give you names of potential employers if you explain that you'd like to meet with them to talk about the career field in general. If you couch your request for names in the context of informational interviewing and general researching of your career field, it sounds like less of a favor. In addition, the person you're talking to will probably feel more comfortable giving you a name and number if it sounds like you would be happy with a general conversation and you won't press your new contact to find you a job.

Keep in mind as you network that a quick and simple meeting or phone conversation is all you're asking for. While it's not that big of a deal for someone to take five minutes to chat with you about career opportunities, it is a big deal if you approach them in an aggressive manner, put them on the spot and demand a job. Again, it's just a question of approach and of not breaking those unspoken job hunting rules. If your professors don't know of anyone personally in your career field, ask them to recommend a few local companies of which they think highly.

Try to get as much practical advice from your professors as you can, such as what to look for in an interview, or how to best establish yourself in your field if you're moving to a new city. For example, professors might know of a professional association that is particularly helpful, or they might have heard horror stories from students who worked as interns for certain companies.

If you know any of your professors well enough, you could ask them to briefly critique your resume. You could almost look at your conversation as a practice networking session. You're learning how to discuss your job hunt with someone in a position of authority, and you're becoming more comfortable with asking for specific suggestions and advice.

You can do all of these things with former employers from a summer job as well. They may be able to steer you towards the job that would be best for you because they are familiar with your work habits.

Family and friends can also be good sources for networking. If a friend of a friend works in the city you'd like to work in, get a name and phone number. Depending upon the age of your potential contact, you could proceed in a couple of different ways.

If the person graduated within the past few years, you could just call, explain that you have a mutual friend, and ask your new contact to go to dinner or lunch. It might be a good way to get all kinds of advice about a new city, and it could help you meet new people your own age.

If the friend of a friend is someone older, you should probably approach your meeting more formally. Send your networking contact your resume and a brief letter stating what kind of job you're interested in. Say you'd like to get together to discuss the job market and get ideas for your job search. Make it clear that you'll get back in touch and then call when you say you will.

"Let's Get Together"

Make it as easy as possible for the person you're contacting to help you out. For example, if your next door neighbor's boyfriend is going to meet with you, don't put the burden of setting up the meeting on him. If getting together with you is too much trouble, he probably won't call you.

After you've reached the person who's going to talk to you, make sure you set up your meeting at a convenient time, date and location. If possible, try to meet with your contact at their office, especially if it is in a field in which you're interested.

If your new contact has time, he or she might give you a brief tour and introduce you to a few of the people in the office. It sounds minor, but it's helpful to see people in your career field in their own office environment. Especially if you can see five or six different companies.

Do the people who have the job you want look rushed? Harried? Are they frequently in meetings? Do they appear to sit in a quiet office and work independently or are they usually interacting with their co-workers? Do they get out and meet with clients and customers? These small glimpses into a real work environment can provide you with the details of what it's like to work in the career field in which you're interested.

It's at this level of networking, trying to utilize existing contacts, that most people our age become discouraged. It's not uncommon to have very few contacts in the job world. Maybe you don't have that many professors you can talk to. Maybe your family and friends don't work in the career field you're interested in and don't know anyone who does.

At this point, you're probably wondering what's wrong with your friends and family members. You can ponder their faults later, but luckily, you can become an incredible networker even if they, and you, don't know a soul.

Networking Through Mass Mailings

The key to making contacts when you don't have any contacts can be found in the second major method of networking, that of sending out mass mailings.

Yes, we're back to mass mailings. In the previous chapter, they may have sounded like a lot of work for a little bit of gain. However, now that you're figuring out how to network, you can see mass mailings in a whole new light. If you've sent out 50 letters to 50 companies and none of them have a job available, you've pretty much wasted your time. Right? Wrong!

Sending out mass mailings is actually only one part of networking, and it can be better defined as "prospecting." Prospecting is the process of finding potential employers with whom you will seek a face-to-face meeting. The face-to-face meeting is the actual networking, but without this first step of "prospecting," many of your networking interviews would not take place.

In other words, mass mailings may not find you a job right away (unless you happen to find companies that are hiring), but this type of prospecting can open the door to a world of networking contacts. Maybe you didn't find any jobs at those 50 companies, but if you've presented yourself well, you've found 50 contacts.

This is where job hunting goes beyond simply being a way to find a job and becomes a way to flesh out your career goals and learn more about what you're looking for in a job. It also becomes a way to build your future. Through mass mailings, you can set up informational interviews.

Informational interviews are another aspect of job hunting that sound worthless. Are they called informational interviews so they can be distinguished from non-informational interviews? Despite their meaningless name, informational interviews are a great way to get your foot in the door.

When you ask for an informational interview, you are indicating to employers that you are only seeking information, and not a job, when you set up an interview. Of course, everyone knows you'd like a job if you could get one, otherwise you would have no interest in the information you're going to obtain. Even though both parties to an informational interview act as though there is no deeper purpose to the meeting than discussing the career field in an abstract sense, informational interviews serve a very real purpose.

"We do conduct informational interviews over the telephone," says The Austin Company's John Stewart. "We realize that things change, and we may not be hiring now, but there may be someone we'd want to court six months from now."

Employers recognize the informational interview as a good way to keep up their contacts with job seekers. However, we once again get into the distinction between large companies and small ones.

As you've gathered by now, large companies follow a fairly rigid set of procedures in hiring. Larger companies are not as likely to talk to job seekers who simply want information. They have highly structured recruitment programs, and they know they can always find a large number of applicants, whether through on-campus interviews or in response to ads in the paper.

GE's Peter Bowen believes that informational interviewing can be good for the job hunter, and he will occasionally meet with recent graduates when he doesn't have a firm opening.

"I'll talk to someone on the phone first," says Bowen, "and if there's some kind of match, I'll meet with an applicant for an informational interview. I do this only on a sporadic basis, however, because I don't have time to do two or three informational interviews a day."

This is not to say that mass mailings or requests for informational interviews are wasted on large companies.

"All it takes is one interview that clicks," comments Chrysler's John Stone. "I don't think most employers have time to do informational interviews, but for those that do, it can be a real asset for job seekers."

Try to structure your job hunt so it fits in with the hiring practices of the companies in which you're interested. If you're interested in larger companies, seeking informational interviews might not be quite as productive for you as other methods of networking. If you're looking at smaller companies, however, informational interviews can be a potential gold mine.

Informational interviews raise the question of which person at a company is best suited to receive your resume. As you can see, when you send out a mass mailing to a small company, you want someone to read it who is in a position to hire you. The first place you might think of would be the personnel office.

However, you also want someone to read your resume who would be interested in helping you network. As we discussed earlier, you are more likely to find this person if you address your letter to the head of the specific department in which you're interested.

Although it seems like companies would have a clear picture of how many employees they need and whether or not they're hiring anyone in the near future, the world is an uncertain place. Things change—employees come and go, corporate budgets rise and fall, consumer demand fluctuates and management strategies are constantly evolving. Just because a company has 30 employees in January and it's not interested in adding to its staff, that doesn't mean it won't suddenly need 50 in July.

The head of each department is aware of this. The personnel office is aware of this also, but they may have other priorities in January besides interviewing someone they may or may not need in July.

From a networking standpoint, a high level executive who works in the area of the company in which you're interested is most likely to take the time to speak to you. As you'll recall, many employers see it as a professional courtesy or a networking responsibility. A lot of people simply like to help younger people get started.

Using Informational Interviews To Your Advantage

After you've obtained an informational interview, you need to figure out what it is that you're going to say. We'll get into all of the tough details of interviewing in the next chapter, such as how to answer difficult questions and how to interact with employers from the moment you walk in the door.

For now, it's sufficient to simply address the general framework of an informational interview, because it is less structured than the standard interview. Most interviews, whether standard or informational, are sort of a give-and-take, with the interviewer telling you what the job involves and asking you what skills you possess.

A good interview is 50-50 because you need to know what an employer would expect of you and the employer needs to know what you're capable of doing. At this point, it may seem now that the only good interview is one that is over, but after we discuss interviewing techniques, you'll feel more confident about the whole process.

Informational interviews are less formal than regular interviews. For one thing, you know that the person who has agreed to speak to you has some interest in helping you climb further up the ladder. They must think you're qualified for the position you're seeking or they wouldn't take the time to talk to you. This makes it easier to jump into an informational interview. Going through informational interviews, in turn, will make it easier for you when you get to your real interviews.

When you go in for an informational interview, be prepared to talk about yourself. It may be as simple as organizing your thoughts before you meet with your contact and determining exactly what kind of position you would like.

Think about what you'd like to do in your job, whether it is advancing the cause an organization represents or learning all about buying network advertising time. You don't need an elaborate game plan for the rest of your life, but you should be prepared to say what it is you want to do and why you think you would be good in the position.

When you go to an informational interview, you should also have some questions prepared. I always hated this part because when I met someone new and talked to them about their job, I was absorbed in what they were saying. My mind, unfortunately, was like a blank slate (probably similar to the way your mind was operating during an eight o'clock class).

When I was in this state of mind and the interviewer would ask if I had any questions, I could only think of things like: Is this carpet grey or more of a slate blue? Where's the bathroom? Why am I here?

You might try to develop a few intelligent questions before you go. For example, it's helpful to find out what people do all day. Ask the interviewer to describe a typical day for you. You might also ask them what qualities the interviewer is looking for in a job applicant or what kind of temperament it takes to do the job and do it well.

These may sound like mundane interview questions, but they have a real purpose. These questions can tell you a lot more about the job for which you're interviewing than can all of the elaborate explanations employers will give you in a "real" interview. In asking what people do in a typical day, you can see what the job is really like.

If an advertising executive says he meets with clients, talks on the phone a lot and meets with the copywriters and design people, you can see if this is the job for you. Maybe you hate detail work and it sounds like he takes care of a tremendous amount of administrative matters. Maybe you thought a person in his position spent a lot of time creating the ads.

Or maybe he does exactly what you thought he did, and you're now more confident in your job search, ready to hone in on exactly the type of job he holds.

As the employer concludes your informational interview,

try to leave with something specific that will help you, whether it is the name of a colleague at another company or some advice on how to improve your resume.

"Get an employer's reaction to your resume," suggests Harrison, "and ask where someone with your background would fit into their organization."

"I Can't Go Out Tonight— I've Got A Meeting"

The third major way to prospect and network is to join every organization you can think of that will advance your job search, whether it's your college alumni club, a professional association of people who work in the field in which you're interested or some kind of social organization, like a fraternity or sorority alumni group.

You need to examine the different types of organizations available to you, and determine which would be most useful for your job search. Professional associations will probably be the most useful, but alumni groups are a close second. If you don't know of any professional groups in your career field, you might call your college's career placement office and ask if they know of the names of these groups. You could also try a former professor, or you could look in the phone book under headings that apply to you.

Every career field has a professional association which members of the industry can join. As we mentioned before, members pay annual dues and are then eligible to attend meetings, seminars, workshops and any other activities put on by the group. Most groups have job banks, or at least informal networking get-togethers, where you can spread the word that you're looking for a job.

Professional associations usually have some kind of publication for their members. If there is a weekly publication, or even one that comes out once a month, check the classifieds in the back of the magazine. You're likely to find some good jobs or at least the names of some potential employers to add to your list of mass mailings.

College and university alumni groups are also a good resource. Many colleges have an established mentor or networking program which joins recent graduates with those who are already established in the field. These networks can be simple, with a mentor and a recent graduate meeting once and talking about the career field, or elaborate, with a mentor keeping in touch with a recent grad throughout the job hunt.

Often, a specific school or field of study within a university will have its own job bank. If you graduated from the journalism school or from the engineering school, for example, you can check and see if there is something designed to help graduates find jobs.

If your alumni group doesn't have anything like this, but it gets together socially, try to attend one of their functions every once in a while. In addition to being a fun way to meet people your age with whom you have something in common, you can learn about job opportunities. You may find out about professional associations you've overlooked, or you could obtain the name of a reliable typesetter for your resume. All of these small things add up, and each piece of useful advice you receive helps you fine tune your job search.

Without going overboard, you could also join a group that has nothing to do with your job search at all, but is simply an area in which you're interested, such as a backpacking club, a book discussion group at a local bookstore or some kind of volunteer organization.

Clearly, if you join an organization which has nothing to do with job hunting, your focus would be different. First, you should only join a group you would actually enjoy being a part of and not one that you would drop out of the first minute you found a job. The purpose in joining some kind of social group is simply to meet as many new people as you can, because you never know who may be aware of a great job opportunity.

As you look for a job, you will soon realize how many other people are looking for jobs or know of jobs that are available. When you meet 25 new people through some kind of social or community group, it's likely that some of them will know of job openings somewhere.

Networking is a funny thing, because all it takes is meeting one person who knows of the perfect job for you. However, you can't predict where you will meet people who can help you in your job hunt, and some of the things you do won't lead you anywhere, except you may have met an interesting person.

Therefore, you should only join these kinds of groups if it's something you'd probably do anyway. Networking should become a way for you to get the most out of all of the activities you do, but it shouldn't become the driving force behind your social life!

"A Job Hunting Seminar— How, Uh, Fun"

Job hunting seminars and resume workshops can also be a good way to network and meet people. You can find all sorts of classes and helpful how-to sessions at local libraries, schools and civic associations. In addition, larger companies sometimes sponsor job fairs.

This may be exactly the type of thing you avoided while

you were in college, but it probably looks more appealing now. At this type of gathering, most of the people you meet will also be looking for jobs, but there are several reasons job hunting seminars can help you out.

First, you might learn something new, whether it's a catchy way to phrase something in your resume or cover letter, another resource for targeting local employers or a suggestion for improving your interviewing skills.

Second, there will be at least one employer or career counselor there. Someone with knowledge of job hunting will be conducting the seminar. Usually, job hunting sessions will include three or four local employers who speak on different aspects of the job hunt.

These are ideal candidates for your networking advances. These people wouldn't participate in this kind of seminar if they didn't find it enjoyable, or if their company wasn't looking for employees at some point. They are likely to be receptive to any networking overtures you might make.

You could simply introduce yourself and ask if you could send them your resume. You could ask if they know of any companies you should include in your job hunt. If the chemistry seems right, you could even ask if you could schedule an appointment to meet with them for five or ten minutes to discuss job hunting.

You can also meet other job seekers at these seminars. This will help you maintain your enthusiasm for the job hunt. It's easy to get discouraged when you look for a job, but when you meet successful, intelligent people who are also unemployed, it helps keep you going. You can start feeling like a lost soul when you're job hunting, and it's always good to commiserate with someone else who may either be confused or discouraged. We'll discuss this more in Chapter 8.

As you network your way to a great job, there are a few things to keep in mind.

It's Up To You

First, networking can do wonders for your job search, but don't expect your professor's colleague or your roommate's dad to just give you a job. Some recent grads expect the people they meet through networking to magically figure out what they're looking for and then go find a range of jobs from which they can choose.

I would get so excited when a person I met through networking would offer to help me out. Two or three times, someone would offer to circulate my resume and make a few calls on my behalf. That would always amaze me, and the temptation was to sit back and let myself believe that this new found contact would do my job hunting for me.

However, you've got to look for a job because no one else is going to do it for you. When it comes down to it, none of the people who help you network care about your finding a job like you do. You're the person to whom it matters the most, and you've got to make sure that you're the person doing the most to find yourself a job.

Second, always follow up on all contacts. If your roommate's brother works at the bank in which you're interested or your cousin's girlfriend runs her own ad agency, get their names and numbers and call them up. Recent graduates often feel embarrassed about networking, but there's nothing wrong with meeting people and telling them you're looking for a job. It's all in how you do it.

You should also follow up on the names which potential employers give you. For example, if you meet with Sue Johnson at ABC Manufacturing and she refers you to Hugh

Smith at Smith Brothers Contracting, schedule a meeting with Hugh Smith, even if it doesn't sound very promising.

You may think that Smith Brothers Contracting is too small or you may be afraid that Hugh Smith doesn't know Sue Johnson as well as she thinks he does. You can have all kinds of doubts as you carry out your job search. In fact, the longer you look for a job, the more you'll tend to doubt your choice of career field, your skills and even your ability to decide what you should eat for breakfast.

Don't let these doubts stop you though. Obtaining a name from a networking source may not seem that important, but you'll never know what you may get out of meeting with someone.

I remember when I dutifully went to speak to a woman who worked for a small public relations firm in New York. She was my roommate's boss' close friend. When I walked into the meeting, I didn't really expect much, because the informational interview had been hastily arranged and I wasn't even all that sure of what I was looking for.

When I walked out of the meeting, I had a job offer, albeit for a temporary three month position as an assistant account executive. I took the job, which, true to my new employer's word, became a permanent post, and I really enjoyed the time I spent working there.

Third, keep everyone who participates in your job hunt informed as to your activities, both in an initial thank you note and through phone calls over the next couple of months.

Thank you notes are not only courteous, they are critical to making a good impression. Thank you notes, like cover letters, can be short and simple. And just as your cover letters basically followed a form letter format, so can your thank you notes.

For example, you might tell Sue Johnson you enjoyed meeting her and you appreciate her taking the time to talk to you about job opportunities. You might mention something specific she did for you, such as critique your resume or suggest a company for you to contact, like Smith Brothers Contracting. When you close your thank you note, tell her that you'll keep in touch and inform her when you get a job.

Then, when you do get a job, follow up on that promise. Write Sue Johnson and all of the other people you met with in the course of your job hunt and tell them who you'll be working for.

Keeping in touch with your networking contacts is a great way to stretch one five minute meeting into a professional relationship. If you meet with Sue Johnson in June and it goes well, you can contact her again in August if you're still looking for a job. You'll have solidified your relationship with her through the thank you note you wrote after your first meeting with her.

If you do call her in August, tell her you wanted to check back and see if she knew of any openings for which you'd be qualified. She may know of the perfect opportunity, but may not have thought of calling you.

As you pursue various leads, make sure that everyone who helps you knows what you're doing. If you keep the people you network with informed as to your progress, they'll be more likely to give you additional names and to take a greater interest in your job hunt.

As you can see, if you network, you'll quickly develop an ever expanding web of contacts. Not only will this make your job search more interesting and more successful, it will make you appreciate your well-organized home office. (Did I just hear you laugh?)

If you've set up your home office, you probably have a Rolodex™, which is the office version of an address book. A good Rolodex™ is a big part of a successful job search. A Rolodex™ is a metal holder which has around three hundred pieces of paper that look like index cards. The cards can be removed and inserted behind permanent cards which each carry a different letter of the alphabet. You should put the name, title, address and phone number of every person you meet on a card in your Rolodex™ and file the cards in alphabetical order.

Clearly, not every person you meet is going to be helpful. But many of the people you meet will be, and it's good to have 10 to 15 people in your Rolodex™ who you can call periodically to see if they either have a job or know of a job.

That may sound like a lot of contacts for someone who just graduated from college, but as you send out mass mailings and network, you will be amazed at the number of people you meet. Keeping track of these people, whether in a Rolodex™ or in a notebook, is a crucial part of networking.

If you'll make the effort to become a successful networker, you'll end up finding a lot more than just a job. You'll learn more about the working world in general and you'll develop a web of professional contacts that will help you move up in your career.

Launching Your Great Enterprise From Small Opportunities

1. Identify any contacts you may already have. You might start by making two lists. Your first list will consist of people you know would be willing to help you, but who may not be connected with your chosen career field. The second list will consist of people you know are connected with your chosen career field, but who may not be willing to help you.

On the first list, write down the names of anyone you would truly feel comfortable asking for help with your job search. You might end up with the names of two or three professors, the parents of a close friend, an old high school teacher and your aunt who lives in another state.

On the second list, write down the names of anyone you can think of in your chosen career field. If you want a job in sales, you might end up with the names of a former neighbor, your friend's sister's husband, a local person who has made it big, and the brother of a person who went to your college or university.

Both of these lists can be useful after you narrow down which of these people would be willing to speak to you. Give yourself two or three days to decide who you will call and what you will say to them.

You can probably take an informal approach with those on your first list. You could simply call or write, tell them you're looking for a job and ask them if they know of anyone you could contact. You should probably take a more formal approach with those on the second list, sending them your resume and a brief letter and asking if they'll meet with you for a few minutes to discuss the field.

2. Follow up on the mass mailings you've sent out. Give yourself a week to call all of the people on your list. Make four or five calls a day. Inquire about the status of your resume and try to set up at least two or three informational interviews.

3. Locate three groups you can join, whether your college alumni group, a social organization with which you have ties from college or a professional association. Ask members of these groups if they know of any other organizations which can help you with your job hunt.

4. Find out about two or three job hunters' seminars.

Check with your local library, call the chamber of commerce or inquire with someone from a professional association.

5. Remember that networking can be a slow but ever-growing process. Keep at it, but don't neglect sending out new letters and responding to new ads. Networking could be a 24-hour-a-day job if you let it be, but remember that you need to keep up with other parts of your job hunt.

6. Once you get your networking under control, you're ready to start thinking about your interviewing strategies. To become more comfortable with the interview process, start reading Chapter 6.

TACKLING INTERVIEWS WITH CONFIDENCE AND POISE...
I Hope I Don't Forget My Name

"As is our confidence, so is our capacity."
—William Hazlitt

Interviews are won on words and wits, on preparation and previous experience—and on first impressions. The interview starts the moment you meet the interviewer and, like it or not, first impressions are vitally important.

"From the first moment they meet you, interviewers know whether or not they want to hire you," says career counselor Sherrie Pavol Bereda of Career Concepts.

You make your first impression on an interviewer in a variety of ways, including the way you're dressed, the way you move, the way you speak and the way you present yourself.

"First impressions are significant," adds General Motors'

James Sturtz, "such as how someone is dressed or how they walk into the room. As an interviewer, the first thing you see is that person. Of course, I do use other information [to judge a job seeker], but personal appearance is important."

Given the importance of first impressions, it's not surprising many recent graduates don't feel entirely confident when they go through that first round of interviews. Interviewing can be an intimidating prospect. However, it doesn't have to be. Most recent graduates see interviews only as a way for an employer to weed out job hunters. What they don't realize, however, is that job hunters are doing some weeding out, and learning, of their own.

"Keep in mind that interviewing is a mutual, reciprocal process," suggests psychologist Dr. Anita Auerbach. "While you're being interviewed, you are also interviewing. You're not sure you will sell your product, yourself, to that company."

The interview is not simply a way for an employer to see if you're the best candidate for the position. It's also a way for you to see if the job is the best one for you—for your personality, your talents, your interests, and your career objectives.

In many ways, an interview is a time for you to interview the employer. It's a time for you to figure out what a company does and what the job you're interviewing for involves. It's a time for you to gather first-hand information about the company so you can decide if you'd like to work there.

"Interviewing is a two way street, and this often isn't as well-recognized by recent graduates," says Chrysler's John Stone. "Recent graduates should remember that they're interviewing to see if the job is something they'd be interested in doing."

When you're interviewing, employers don't hold your future in their hands—you do. This can be a reassuring thought. And it can lead to more successful, and even enjoyable, interviews. If you'll remember that you will eventually find a job, you'll see that each interview isn't a do-or-die situation. Every interview is important, but if your meeting with one employer doesn't go well, you will have other opportunities to present yourself in a favorable light.

A lot of recent grads don't really believe this. They feel trapped and desperate. They blow interviews out of proportion, and they don't realize the ways in which they can use an interview to learn more about potential employers.

"Often, recent college graduates fall into the 'I need a job syndrome,'" says Stone.

Shaken job hunters who fall into this trap believe that if they do well in the interview, they'll get a job and their lives might possibly go on. If they don't do well in the interview, they will never find a job, and they will die an agonizing death, perhaps even during the interview itself. Not, of course, that I have experienced this myself.

While there are clearly some wrong ways to interview, there is no one right way. This sounds discouraging until you think about it. What it really means is that as long as you avoid specific interviewing mistakes, you're free to act and speak as you wish. Within the normal bounds of acceptable dress and behavior, you can, and should, talk, dress and act in a way that reflects your individual style and personality.

Every interview is different, depending upon the personalities involved. If John the Job Hunter meets with Mr. Employer before you do, John will answer all of the questions in a different way than you will. He will dress differently, and he will mention different activities on his resume.

When you walk into the interviewer's office and interview differently from the way John did, neither one of you is wrong.

Unless, of course, John the Job Hunter knocked over Mr. Employer's priceless antique vase or you happen to be wearing those great new hiking boots you got last week. In that case, you're both in trouble.

To be on the safe side, we'll use this chapter to point out all of the wrong ways of interviewing. If you can avoid making the mistakes we discuss here, you can interview with confidence and poise, because you'll know that what you're doing is right.

We'll also look at what you should do before, during, and after the interview. At this point, that probably covers all of your waking hours. But if you'll look at each stage of interviewing before you get started, you'll be able to use interviews to your greatest advantage and with the least amount of anxiety.

What Not To Do During Your Interview

It may sound negative to begin with a list of what not to do during an interview, but it's actually the easiest way to prepare yourself. If you have a firm understanding of what creates a poor first impression, you're one step ahead of the hapless soul who wanders in completely unprepared.

If you want to make a positive first impression, be sure NOT to dress inappropriately, communicate poorly or ask the wrong questions at the wrong time. You may wish you could have given these guidelines to your first college date. Avoiding these mistakes is easier said than done, right? We'll get into specifics in this chapter.

These are broad categories, but employers stress that most interview mistakes fall into one of these three areas. If you start out with a clear idea of what to avoid, you can proceed with confidence.

"What Should I Wear?"

Yes, we're back to my initial job hunting obsession, that of what to wear to an interview. The clothing issue sounds trivial, but Stone believes it reflects applicants' overall judgment and their level of understanding of the job hunting process.

"The first thing that strikes me is whether a candidate is dressed appropriately," says Stone.

What you wear to an interview greatly influences an interviewer's perception of you. It's not that you have to look stunningly attractive or even all that fashionable. Instead, you need to avoid looking underdressed, sloppy or out of place. In interviewing, being underdressed can potentially eliminate you from getting the job.

"One mistake I see a lot of recent graduates make is that they have too casual an appearance," says Perpetual Bank's Terri Goslin-Jones. "Anyone looking for a job should always dress professionally. That means no sports coats and no dresses."

The good news about this particular interviewing mistake is that it is easy to prevent. As long as you wear traditional, conservative interview clothes, you will be dressed appropriately, even if you're not a traditional, conservative person or the job is not a traditional, conservative job. Save the wacky clothes that express your inner being for the weekends, and be content to let your personality shine through from what you are saying, not from what you are wearing.

Men may find the question of what to wear to an interview slightly less confusing than women. Women, after all, have more options, from suits to dresses to skirts and blouses. However, to be on the safe side, women should go with suits and avoid frilly dresses or flimsy blouses.

"Suits for women are not required per se, but it is essential that they're dressed in a manner consistent with the business environment," says Stone. "An interview is not a cocktail hour, a party or church."

In general, women should wear a suit, a good blouse and standard pumps. Men should wear a conservative wool suit with a traditional tie and the appropriate dress shoes.

"Job hunters should look the role even before they get the job," career counselor Marilyn Goldman of Horizons Unlimited explains.

Women should take these words to heart in terms of their make-up as well. If you don't wear make up, that's fine. If you do, you should probably wear what you'd wear during the day on campus, and avoid anything you'd wear for parties or for going out at night.

The second part of dressing to make a good first impression involves how you look in your clothes. Avoid looking wrinkled, messy or generally unkempt. The fact that some of your friends spent four years of college wearing clothes that had been rolled up on the floor of their closet can sort of warp your perspective. I'd rule out that wrinkled look, as well as the wardrobe composed entirely of sweats and t-shirts with obscene logos.

"You Mean I Can't Do My Beaver Imitation?"

As interviewers form that vital first opinion of you, they are looking at more than your clothes. They also want to see how well you interact with people and how friendly you are.

How you greet the interviewer, therefore, contributes to the first impression you make. If you wander weakly into the room and just stand there, or if you rush clumsily into the room, and look flustered and out of breath, you probably won't make a great first impression. Of course, anyone would be out of breath if they had gotten trapped in the stairwell, climbed fourteen flights of stairs and had an anxiety attack before the interview, but it's probably better not to bring that up.

When you go in for an interview, remember that you should make as much of an effort as the interviewer does to see that things go smoothly. If you think about making things easier for the interviewer, what to do in each part of the interview will become more clear. For example, is it easier for the interviewer if you stand there silently without any kind of expression on your face, or if you walk in, smile pleasantly, and say, "Hello, my name's John Smith"?

If you're ever in doubt as to how to proceed during an interview, try to make the situation more comfortable. Any kind of polite effort on your part will be well-received. This, in turn, will make you feel more confident.

In addition to good manners, employers are looking for poise and self-possession. The best way to appear self-possessed is to introduce yourself when you enter the room and speak up whenever you're asked a question. You don't have to act like Mr. Charm or Miss Personality. As long as you are clearly making an effort to keep the interview rolling, the interviewer will see you in a positive light.

Stone likes to see job hunters make an effort to introduce themselves. "The second thing that I notice in forming a first impression, after how someone is dressed," says Stone, "is how they introduce themselves. I also notice whether or not they smile."

Much of this detail about interviewing may sound insignificant, and certainly not related to any job skills. However, how well you mix with people can be integral to many jobs. In providing advice about interviewing, employers stress that they want candidates who can communicate effectively with other people and represent the company well.

"It's very important that the people we hire can communicate well," says General Electric's Peter Bowen.

Communication skills are a broad category, and it can be hard to have a clear picture of what employers mean when they say they're turned off by someone who communicates poorly. What they mean by a poor communicator is someone who is hard to talk to and who doesn't seem to be trying to keep up his or her part of the interview.

"One mistake that recent graduates frequently make is not looking an interviewer in the eye and not speaking clearly," explains Pavol Bereda.

It's important to maintain eye contact with interviewers. Several employers mentioned that they form a negative impression of a person who can't look at them directly during the interview.

"A lot of people look at the ability to maintain eye contact as a source of strength and of being able to communicate effectively," comments Ford's Darrell Washington.

Again, it's a minor point, but if interviewers start feeling a growing sense of irritation because you keep staring at the floor or at an imaginary spot on the wall, you'll eventually lose their interest. Like anyone else, interviewers are going to be most interested in the person who is easiest to talk to and easiest to deal with. You may simply be nervous, but don't let small issues like physical mannerisms sabotage your interview.

Another part of communicating effectively is answering the questions that are asked of you. IBM's Colette Abissi, based in Armonk, New York, sees two mistakes that many recent graduates make when it comes to following a line of questioning. First, says Abissi, job seekers often ramble and provide answers which are not related to the question. Second, they provide short, yes/no answers that don't give the interviewer any insight into their personality or qualifications. Both mistakes can be big ones.

"Keep your answers focused, and make sure you're answering the question that was asked of you," advises Abissi. "Try not to ramble and lose focus."

When trying to avoid the first problem, that of losing sight of the question asked of you, try to answer all questions with specific examples. You might be able to keep on the subject if you relate all of the questions you're asked to something on your resume. If you're asked how you work under pressure, give a concrete example of what you did in a specific situation, whether it was during a crisis at a summer job or in meeting a particularly difficult academic deadline.

Abissi also sees recent college graduates miss opportunities to describe themselves, their work experiences and their ambitions. "I've seen job hunters answer a question in one or two words when it would have been to their advantage to elaborate."

For example, if you worked in a book store one summer, and the interviewer asked if you liked it, you shouldn't just say yes. Say what the challenges were, what you learned from the experience, how you benefited and if the job had any impact on your future career decisions.

"Most interview questions require more than a yes/no answer," adds Pavol Bereda. "You've got to sell yourself."

"Maybe I Shouldn't Have Brought That Up"

Finally, interviewers said they're turned off by job hunters who ask the wrong questions at the wrong time, such as inquiring too early about salary and benefits. Benefits include vacation and sick days, health insurance, and any perks like free parking or the use of a company gym.

Most employers and career counselors don't think you should bring up salary or benefits during the first interview. If you're interviewing with a small company or with one that is in a rush to fill a position, you may only have one interview. In this case, the interviewer is likely to bring up the subject of salary and benefits near the end of the interview. Therefore, there isn't any real point in introducing the subject into the interview until the employer does. In your first interview with a particular employer, stay away from any questions that don't relate to the job or the company.

Now that we've looked at what you shouldn't do, let's talk about what you should do. This may seem a little more confusing because it's not as clear-cut, but that simply gives you the freedom to be yourself.

What To Expect

First, most interviews will last anywhere from fifteen minutes to half an hour. However, the length of time you're interviewing doesn't mean anything. Don't feel you've failed if the interview lasts less than ten minutes. It could be that the person you've met with does everything at a rapid pace and knows how to find exactly what he's looking for in a few minutes. Conversely, don't think you'll definitely get the job if someone talks to you for an hour. Everyone has a different pace. Unfortunately, there aren't any secret signals that can let you know whether you'll be offered the job.

Second, most interviews follow a straightforward format, with the interviewer dividing the time evenly between asking you about yourself and telling you about the job. Some interviewers like to tell you all about the job first and then ask you questions second. Some like to begin by asking you about your credentials and then telling you what they're looking for. It's a little easier if they do the talking first and then ask you questions later, but don't be thrown off by an interview that starts with questions from the beginning.

Third, interviewing is simply an extension of your resume and your cover letter. When you wrote your cover letters, you tried to use each sentence and each paragraph to promote yourself. You used your cover letter to emphasize your interest in the company and your particular skills. You also used it to differentiate yourself from other job applicants. You can do that with the interview as well.

"In an interview, you have to prove that you will be an asset to the company," says Pavol Bereda. "It's important that you sell yourself and make the employer want to hire you."

However, be sure you do this in a sincere way.

Before The Interview

There are several ways to prepare for an interview. First, you can research the companies that have jobs available. Second, you can identify three of your strengths and figure out how to communicate them to the interviewer. Third, you can familiarize yourself with frequently asked interview questions. Fourth, you can practice your answers to these questions aloud.

You have two options regarding your pre-interview research. As we've discussed before, you can learn as much as possible about each individual company with which you're interviewing. Or, you can practice what you're going to say and how you're going to answer tough questions, regardless of the company with which you're interviewing. The method you choose will depend upon how much time you have available.

Taking the first approach, that of learning as much as you can about an individual company, can help you make a better impression on the interviewer. It can help you make decisions about whether you want to work at a particular company, and it can help you feel comfortable and more relaxed during your interview. I know, you'd probably rather use this new found information to impress people at cocktail parties, because at this stage of the game, anything seems better than interviewing.

"In order to help you desensitize for an interview," says psychologist Dr. Auerbach, "look into what a company does. This will enhance your self-confidence and give you a sense that you've got something to offer."

Learning about a company before an interview will prevent you from making an embarrassing mistake, such as not knowing what kind of product the company manufactures or not knowing that it was involved in a highly publicized labor dispute.

To find out more about the companies with which you will be interviewing, call their public affairs office to ask for a copy of their annual report or for product literature. You can say you're interested in learning more about the company, and you'd like any information that is available.

You can also go to the library and scan the periodicals guide to see if there were any articles about the company in the newspaper in the past year. You can learn about the company's financial performance or about the role it plays in your community.

It is fairly easy to do this type of research when you're interviewing with a major corporation or a large local employer. It can be a little more difficult to research smaller companies.

When researching smaller companies, you can call the public affairs office and ask for information on the company, just as you did with a larger employer. If the company doesn't have a formal public affairs office, you might call the receptionist and tell her you'd like information. You can ask what the organization does, how long it has been in business and if it has any offices elsewhere.

However, this one-on-one research can be time-consuming. This probably isn't the kind of advice the experts want to hear anyone give, but I wouldn't engage in in-depth research of a company unless it is a big corporation or it has a reputation for being a stickler about details.

If you're interviewing with a smaller or less traditional company, you can probably bypass in-depth research. The advantage of avoiding individual research is that you won't be spending time in preparation that will advance your cause with only one company.

If you are interviewing with a large corporation, though, you would be wise to invest your time in personalized research. Larger companies place greater emphasis on applicants being familiar with daily business operations. Finding out more about a large company prior to your interview might make the difference between a successful interview and a lackluster one.

The second method of interview preparation can help you in every interview you have, regardless of who the employer is. This preparation involves yourself, and it doesn't require as much time. It only requires an understanding of the interview process and a few hours of practice.

Studying a list of typical interview questions may not sound necessary, but many people get nervous when they interview. And many people completely lose their cool when they get nervous. After these people (neither you nor I, of course) get themselves into a nervous state during an interview, they can't concentrate or follow what someone else is saying.

To avoid joining the ranks of recent graduates scarred by traumatic interview experiences, familiarize yourself with the typical questions that interviewers ask. This way, you won't be knocked off balance by difficult or unexpected questions. You can then develop well-organized answers. You can also make a lasting impression on the interviewer.

This sounds kind of daunting, but it's as simple as having the interviewer think, "He is intelligent, motivated and a nice guy," when you walk out the door. Or having the interviewer think, "She is well-organized, assertive, and an independent thinker."

You want the interviewer to form some kind of impression of you to differentiate you from other applicants who may come across as being dull or colorless. To guard against not making any kind of impression on the interviewer, you should go into the interview prepared to talk about your three primary strengths or impressive achievements.

These points will be different for each person, but they don't have to be anything startling or exotic. Think of your strengths, both as a person and as a prospective employee. What would you like to communicate about these strengths to the interviewer? How would these traits, characteristics or achievements tie in with the job you're seeking?

If you're honest, imaginative, articulate, inventive, aggressive or cool under pressure, make that known. If you graduated with a 4.0, won a prize from a literary magazine, had an amazing summer internship or saved 500 trees on campus through an environmental project, make that known. Whatever it is that makes you distinctive and unique, pass that on to the interviewer.

It's easy to come up with three points that will set you apart, but it can be difficult to know how to utilize them. To help you make a lasting impression on the interviewer, look over the interview questions below. Figure out where you can work in your three unique points.

"But That Question Isn't On My List!"

1. Tell me a little bit about yourself.
2. Did you like your college? What were some of your favorite classes? Why?
3. What was your biggest accomplishment in college? your biggest disappointment?
4. If you had to go to college all over again, would you do anything differently?
5. What are your strengths and weaknesses?
6. How would a previous employer describe you?
7. Why do you want to work here?
8. What do you know about the company?
9. How does your previous experience relate to the job we have available?
10. Why have you been looking for a job for such a long time?

These questions can give you a general idea as to the types of things an employer would like to learn about you. Employers ask questions like these during an interview because they want to know more about your personality and your work habits. They don't expect something witty, catchy or amusing from you every time you open your mouth. Instead, they want to see how well you'd fit into their organization.

A lot of job hunting comes down to personality. That's not to say you have to possess blinding charisma or charm. It simply means that an employer, consciously or unconsciously, will select someone she likes. She will also select a person she thinks is similar to the other people who work there. Or, if she's trying to change the overall feel of the department, she'll select a person different from the people who work there in order to shake up the organization or restructure the division.

In short, employers make all kinds of decisions based upon your personal attributes, and you have no way of knowing exactly what they're looking for. Therefore, when you interview, while you're trying to present your best self to the employer, you also need to present your real self. This way, employers can be sure of what it is that they're getting, and you can be sure you've got the right qualities for the job.

This is an important point. You're not practicing your responses to interview questions so that you can pretend you're something you're not. Instead, you're trying to communicate your strong points. If you present yourself as something other than what you are, and you do it successfully, you will end up getting a job that requires the skills of this person that you made up to impress the interviewer and not the skills that you really possess. With this in mind, let's look at some good responses to the following typical interview questions.

1. Tell me a little bit about yourself.

This is probably the hardest interview question ever invented because it is so vague. The best way to answer the seemingly innocuous tell-me-about-yourself question is to start with the bare facts.

You could say, "As you can see, I majored in physics at the University of Arizona, and I graduated with a 3.7. I'm interested in a job in product design, and I believe my course work ties in well with the position your company is advertising."

You can then discuss one or two of your courses and say what you enjoyed most about them. Depending upon the interviewer, you can give a fairly lengthy answer. The key to answering an open-ended interview question is not to rush through it.

If interviewers want to talk to you about something else, they'll guide you that way. You might start by talking about your physics class and they might ask you if you took any humanities courses and if you have any other interests outside of physics. (Hopefully, you do.) Good interviewers will direct your conversation. If there's something specific they want to know, they'll ask you outright or lead the interview in that direction.

Probably the worst thing you can do with open-ended questions is to become flustered and clam up. When interviewers ask you to tell them about yourself and you say that you'd like to work there and then you sit there silently, several things will happen, all of which are bad.

First, you will become nervous and tongue-tied. It will be difficult to spit out the answer to any question. The interviewer will have to start pounding you with question after question in order to keep the conversation going, and you'll lose sight of the points you'd like to get across.

Second, the interviewer will think you communicate poorly or that you're unresponsive or disinterested. When you answer a tell-me-about-yourself question, take the time to put your answer together before you start to speak.

You may find open-ended interview questions difficult to answer because there are so many things you could talk about. Do interviewers want to know about your academic experience? Your summer jobs? Where you're from? What you're like as a person? Why you want to work at their company? They probably want to know something about each of these things. If you've started with the bare facts and the interviewer seems to want you to continue, you can briefly begin to list your personal characteristics. The key here is not to be too personal. For example, if you were a counselor at a summer camp for three years, you could say this was a valuable experience for you because you love sports and you enjoy working with kids. Maybe you come from a large family and there were always lots of kids around.

It's fine for you to mention these things because it gives the interviewer a better sense of you as a person. From a strict job hunting standpoint, it's not really relevant, so you don't want to spend too much time talking about personal things. Telling an interviewer something about yourself, however, can lighten the atmosphere and make the interviewer more interested in you as an individual.

However, don't talk about anything too intimate. Don't talk about your love life, don't talk about what you did a few evenings ago, don't complain about the city you live in and don't talk about your problems. If you're in doubt as to whether something is too personal, think about whether you'd want it written down for another person to read.

Many interviewers will take notes while you're talking. They will use these notes to refresh their own memories or to pass their impressions on to their supervisors. If you start talking about your crazy roommate, or your break-up with your beloved during college, you probably aren't bringing up the best subjects.

However, there are positive ways to introduce personal details into the interview. For example, you might explain that you'd like to be a teacher because your life was affected deeply by one of your teachers when you were young.

When interviewers ask you to tell them about yourself, they don't want you to boast about your intellect, your leadership abilities or your incredible popularity on campus.

But since you've prepared in advance, you know that you're going to work one or two of your accomplishments into the conversation if it fits.

For example, you can say that majoring in chemistry was exciting because you were selected by the chairman of the department to work on a unique research project. Or that you've always been interested in traveling internationally because you speak three languages. Or that you're eager to get involved with a job in which you interact with other people because you learned so much serving as the president of two major campus organizations.

You don't have to lay it on too thick. The employer is probably aware of most of your achievements because you have mentioned them in your resume and your cover letter. However, you should never pass up the opportunity to say something positive about yourself during an interview. You're the only one who can point out your accomplishments, and as long as you bring out your strong points in a way that flows naturally in the conversation, you won't sound arrogant or egotistical.

2. Did you like your college? What were your favorite classes?

Employers would like to know how you did in school and why you're interested in your particular major. This is a good time to relate your major to the job you're looking for, particularly if it appears to be unrelated. Although it is hard to understand why anyone would think the study of modern sculpture is not related to a job in product research.

If your major ties in well with the job you're seeking, elaborate on how instructive your class work was. Express your eagerness to learn more about the field, and ask a question or two about the approach that the company favors.

If your major doesn't tie in with the job, you can proceed in two ways. If it's not that different, explain why you chose to major in what you majored in and not the more obvious major for the particular job for which you're interviewing. You can be honest. If you weren't originally interested in the field, tell the interviewer what changed your mind. Talk about the particular area of the field in which you'd like to work, and discuss one or two of your personality traits that make you well-suited for the job.

For example, you might say you're interested in accounting because it plays such a critical role in the daily management of a company. You could point out that you're detail-oriented and able to concentrate on difficult subjects for hours at a time. You might not want to mention that you frequently get lost trying to find your own apartment or that you have a hard time remembering your best friend's last name.

After all that we've said about honesty, if you didn't like school, this is an area you may need to be less than forthcoming about. Employers are not going to be impressed by job seekers who didn't care about their classes, their major or their academic performance. If your classes bored you, you shouldn't admit that. Find something about your classes that you liked or some area of your major in which you did well and talk about the challenges it presented you.

If your grades were not particularly good, this is the time to deal with the subject. As we discussed in the chapter on cover letters, mention some other area in which you excelled. Point out how well you did in some other academic area, or mention if your grades progressively improved. If there was some kind of extenuating circumstance, like you were working full-time or you were ill one year, touch on that briefly, but don't make it sound like you're making excuses for yourself. Acknowledge your poor grades and move on to discussing the more positive aspects of your college career.

3. What was your biggest accomplishment in college? your biggest disappointment?

This almost gets into the realm of cute and pointless interview games. We'll discuss later in this chapter what to do if your interview degenerates into a challenge of wits between yourself and the interviewer. For now, let's look at how to answer difficult or unusual questions in a way that promotes your skills and demonstrates your interests.

Talking about your accomplishments, and yes, your disappointments, gives you another opportunity to bring up your three strong points. Mention the classes you took, grades you earned, awards you won or even interesting friends you met. Again, you can be a little personal if it offers a glimmer into your true self or your over-all work habits.

When you answer this question about achievements and disappointments, try to put things in a positive light. Surprisingly, you can do this with your disappointments, too. Your ability to answer even hard interview questions with positive statements will separate you from other job seekers.

The trick here is to be selective in the disappointments you share with the interviewer. You don't have to tell an interviewer anything you don't want to. While the core of any interview is honesty on both sides, it is to some degree a game. If your biggest college disappointment is too personal to get into, don't feel compelled to discuss it. Or if your biggest college disappointment sounds trivial, even though it really disappointed you, discuss a disappointment that reveals something positive about you.

Maybe your biggest disappointment was a social one, like

you weren't able to have the roommate you wanted junior year or you didn't make the final cut for a popular performing arts group on campus. It might serve you better to talk about an academic disappointment, such as not having a paper you wrote accepted for a prestigious campus review or not taking a class from a science professor who went on to receive a presidential award for his teaching. Mentioning these disappointments indicates that you cared about your major and your grades.

You can mention social disappointments, or those that came in your extracurricular activities, only if they can be used to demonstrate that you're an active go-getter. For example, if you ran for president of your student government and lost, mention that.

The best way you can score points on your college disappointments answer is to bring up situations in which you were disappointed and you did something to change whatever caused your disappointment. Maybe you didn't make the Dean's List freshman year so you studied diligently the remaining three years and you came out at the top of your class. Or you didn't win the presidency of the student government so you formed a student coalition to rejuvenate the honor system.

Unfortunately, we often suffer disappointments which only make us disappointed, rather than spur us on to some kind of noble, impressive achievement. If you can't think of a genuine disappointment that led you to accomplish something, mention a situation that wasn't really a disappointment, but subtly brings up one of your strong points.

For example, maybe one of the three points that you want to leave with an interviewer is that you organized a fund raising drive on campus for a local charity. You could say you were disappointed that you weren't able to be in charge of the fund raiser for all four years because there was so much more you could have accomplished.

If you played a role in developing an important program on campus, talk about it. For example, if as a senior you served as an adviser to freshman and you brought 50 other seniors in to help with the program, you could say you were disappointed that you didn't think of doing it earlier.

You get the idea. Use the conversation about disappointing events to talk about your achievements. Just don't lay it on too thick, or you will sound cocky and insincere.

4. If you had to go to college all over again, would you do anything differently?

Your first reaction may be "who cares?" It doesn't seem terribly important, but it's another way for an interviewer to get a sense of you as a person.

First, this question and the preceding one can demonstrate if a job applicant is an obnoxious, complaining whiner. You know the type. It's the person for whom nothing is ever good enough, fun enough or what it was cracked up to be. People like this can have a heyday with any question involving disappointment or introspective thought.

Second, interviewers ask questions like this to see if you approach your life in a thoughtful manner or if you just roll along with whatever comes your way. Even if you don't think you'd do anything differently, you should probably say you would and then list a few examples.

Interviewing involves a lot of subjective judgments. Even though you have a right to approach life any way you want to, most interviewers are looking for a somewhat idealized person, at least in the interview stage. They want someone who fits the popular notion of success. If you are a happy-go-lucky person who doesn't worry about the future or reflect on the past, it would probably benefit you to act as though you do.

When answering this question, bring up one of your three strong points. For example, if you made great grades, say that if you had to do it all over again, you would take the time to tutor your peers who were struggling. If you were an amazing organizer, say you would have shuffled around your commitments and used your talents to help out the sailing club. It doesn't have to be anything big, as long as it demonstrates your skills.

If your answer to the question of what you would do differently is a negative one, make it positive. If you would have gone to another school, chosen another major or participated in an entirely different set of campus activities, that's O.K., but don't talk about it in a negative fashion. Your answer should reflect that you've learned a little bit about life and you're willing to correct your mistakes.

5. What are your strengths and weaknesses?

I'm sure you'll be surprised to learn what you should talk about to describe your strengths! Yes, your three points. And your weaknesses? You have two options here. You can either go with pseudo weaknesses, like you did in answering the disappointments question, or you can go with real weaknesses and demonstrate how you overcame them.

First, for the strengths. You're probably starting to see that you've got all of the perfect interview responses inside you as long as you take the right approach. An interview is basically a way to reiterate your strengths and minimize your weaknesses, no matter what question you're asked. It's nice to be asked about your strengths outright because it doesn't take as much effort to work them into the conversation.

So for your strengths, discuss your three points. Mention the interesting things on your resume. Prepare for this question by making sure you can describe your strengths in one or two paragraphs. Always include specific examples which demonstrate your good points.

As far as your weaknesses go, you're probably getting the hang of talking about things that aren't really all that bad. We all have weaknesses, and some of our weaknesses are worse than others. Talk about your minor weaknesses.

It's probably not good to mention that you procrastinate so badly that you're always in trouble in some area of your life. However, you could admit that you often commit to too many projects at one time and end up working twice as hard in order to pull everything off. As weaknesses go, that's not such a bad one.

Or you can take a slightly more honest approach and mention a genuine weakness and then tell how you get around it.

"When someone asks you what one of your weaknesses is, you can deal with it by pointing out how you compensate for it," says career counselor Susan Schubert of Schubert & Associates. "You could say, 'I'm not good at detail work, so I make a schedule and I take care of details at a specific time.'"

6. How would a previous employer describe you?

This is a cross between a strength-and-weakness question and a tell-me-about-yourself question. You probably know what types of things a previous employer would say about you. When you describe yourself through her eyes, try to be specific. Don't say, "Oh, I think she'd say I worked hard" or "She'd call me responsible and serious."

Instead, point to a specific experience. Say that your boss was pleased by your willingness to stay late every day for a month when the company was in a crunch, and from that experience, you think she would describe you as being diligent, a team player and someone who works well under pressure.

7. Why do you want to work here?

This can be a difficult question. Basically you want a job and this particular company has one open. However, this isn't good enough. Interviewers like to feel that you have a personal interest in their company above all of the other companies with which you've been interviewing.

The best thing you can do is summarize your related experience, whether from your classes or from a summer job, and express your interest in learning more about the field. If you're interviewing for a civil engineering job, you can say it looks similar to the work to which you were exposed during a summer internship. You can mention that you like working independently and that you enjoy being outdoors.

It's probably not good to talk specifically about the company unless you've done some research and you know something about it. If you say that it would mean a lot to you to work for ABC Manufacturing, that might lead to questions like, "What specifically do you like about ABC Manufacturing?" or "What do you know about our company?"

8. What do you know about our company?

Well, here it is. The big fact question. You either know something or you don't, and it's a little bit harder to give pseudo answers. Luckily, I never found this question that hard because interviewers never seemed to pursue it too much. It probably depends upon the size and type of company with which you're interviewing, but a fairly short answer is likely to suffice.

When I was first looking for a job, I was interviewing with ad agencies. It wasn't too hard to list a few of their clients or talk about how creative a certain ad was. To be honest, you can often learn something about a company just by sitting in their office. Many offices will put up awards they've won from certain organizations or commendations they've received for community service.

Clearly, if they've put an award or certificate in their reception area, it's important to them. Keep a sharp eye out and read anything you can while you're waiting for the interviewer to meet with you. Then, in your interview, mention that you know the company has won special recognition for its concern for the environment or for donating its surplus products to the needy or whatever it is the company has done. You don't need to say that you know about this only because you read a plaque in the lobby.

However, as we've mentioned, you might want to invest in some more intensive research if you're interviewing with a major corporation or if you've been called back for a second interview.

9. How does your previous experience relate to the job we have available? What makes you a good candidate for the job?

You have several options in answering this question. You can either relate one or two work experiences, classes or special projects to the job, or you can talk about abstract qualities, like your public speaking ability or your talent for planning corporate events. If you can, point out similarities between your summer jobs and the job you're interested in. Anything you can do to emphasize your previous experience will help you win the job.

The second question, that of what makes you a good candidate, is another version of the first, but it can catch job hunters off guard because it is somewhat vague. Each time interviewers ask you a question about your skills or your worth as an employee, start at the beginning of your resume and briefly sum up everything you have done. This will give you time to collect your thoughts and think of another way to sell yourself.

Questions about your qualifications can be intimidating because they almost sound like a challenge. Depending upon how the interviewers ask you, it can sound like they don't think you're qualified. This probably isn't the case. Interviewers want to hear you specifically relate your skills to the job. They also want to see how much you know about the job.

10. Why have you been looking so long?

If you have been looking for a job for a while, employers might ask you why it has taken you so long. Schubert advises that you be prepared for this question, and have a few specific reasons.

"You might say that it is a tight market, and you could give some examples of what you've been doing," says Schubert. "You could say that you've gone on X number of interviews or that you've been researching a variety of companies. Make it clear that you've been looking."

If you want to put it in a more positive light, you could say something about there being a lot of opportunities, and you want to make sure you find the job that is right for you.

Practicing Your Response

The final part of your interview preparation involves practicing aloud with a friend. This is the step you're most likely to neglect, and, once you get into the interview, the step you're most likely to regret not having done before.

You can have a great set of answers to interview questions in your mind, but if you've never articulated these answers, you can have a hard time getting it all said during your first interview. If you haven't heard yourself respond to questions out loud, you might not realize how long it takes you to come to the point. Or how often you repeat yourself. Or how uncertain you sound when you talk about your strong points. Or how you keep saying "Um" and "You know" every couple of sentences.

"One thing that is helpful is to role play," advises Dr. Diane Goebes. "Get a good friend to be a personnel director and ask questions. Have your friend hold a clipboard and put a little pressure on you."

However, don't blow your minor interviewing flaws out of proportion. Interviewers realize that you may be feeling anxious. They won't penalize you for acting like a normal human being.

"We recognize that people are nervous when they come to interviews," says Bowen. "If I can tell someone is nervous, I'll back off a little bit, maybe by changing the subject for a while and talking about something else."

Practicing aloud before you go to an interview can get rid of those last minute fears and help you come across smoothly. It can also help you learn to talk about yourself.

"People underestimate the value of behavioral rehearsal," comments Dr. Auerbach. "In general, the more you practice something, the better you will be at it, and it will seem less frightening."

You can also use an informal practice session with a friend to see what interviewers see when they look at you. Interview your friend, and notice how he or she answers questions. Think about your friend's strong points and weak points and see how you compare.

"Practice not being the candidate, but being the interviewer," says Schubert. "Make up a job, think about what you're looking for and interview a friend."

This way, you can see how you would expect someone to answer a question about skills or past experiences. It might become obvious to you that interviewers would like to hear about your classes when they ask one question. Or about your campus activities when they ask another because that is how you'd expect someone to answer if you were asking the questions.

In addition, you'll see that anyone can interview if he or she is prepared. As long as job seekers keep the conversational ball rolling and don't stray from the subject, the interviewers can get a picture of an applicant's personality and career goals.

What To Do During Your Interview

At the end of the interview, the employer will ask if you have any questions. If you didn't think of anything during the interview, this is the time to pull out the standard questions you ask each interviewer.

You have two objectives in asking questions. The first is to demonstrate your understanding of the job to the interviewer and to express your interest in the company. The second is to obtain information that will help you make a decision as to whether the company is a place you'd like to work.

The questions that you ask are important, but they don't need to be unique, probing, or earth shattering. Simple questions about the company's objectives for a new product line or its success with a recent expansion are sufficient. You might ask why the company chose a particular year to introduce an innovative new program or what kinds of conditions it looks for before making a major move.

Or, if you're looking for a job in sales, you can ask about the level of individual interaction between sales reps and clients. If you're looking for a job as a fund raiser for a nonprofit organization, you can ask what type of spokesperson the company has had the greatest success with in its fund raising campaigns. Asking intelligent questions can distinguish you from other applicants and point to your knowledge of the job for which you're applying.

If you can't think of anything to ask about the specific company with which you're interviewing, ask questions that would directly affect you. Ask about the job and how the interviewer would describe the work environment. As we mentioned in the previous chapter, you should ask what type of person the employer is looking for and what qualities the ideal applicant would possess. This can reveal to you whether you're the right person for the job.

For example, I once interviewed for a job I thought I really wanted. When I asked what kind of person the employer was looking for, I realized with regret that it wasn't the job for me. The employer wanted someone who was very tough, able to wheel and deal and negotiate with others in the company. The ideal candidate would be outspoken, aggressive, and ready to jump in and fight for what he or she believed. I was none of those things.

However, the employer was not aware of this because I am talkative and outgoing. I could probably have persuaded him that I was the best person for the job, but if I had gotten this job, I would have been miserable. You can therefore learn a lot from the questions you ask, and it's wise to get as much information as you can from each interview.

When you're asking questions to find out what the job is really like, ask who you would report to directly if you were to get the job. Ask how the office is structured. Would you be working independently or on group projects? Would you be required to give presentations to others in the department? Would you be required to travel? Is there much overtime?

These last two questions are tricky because you don't want to make yourself sound lazy. It gets back to the major interviewing mistake of asking the wrong questions at the wrong time. However, you need to know these things if you're going to make an informed decision.

If you ask about things like travel and overtime near the end of the interview in an unemotional way, you're not likely to offend the interviewer. You'll need to judge each individual interview to see when it's appropriate to ask these questions.

In general, it is fine to ask questions about aspects of the job which would have a very real impact on you. If interviewers can tell that you only want a job that involves travel, and their job doesn't, or that you don't want a job that requires a lot of overtime, and their job does, it's better to get weeded out now than to end up in a job in which you wouldn't be satisfied. We'll get into this more in the chapter on decision making, but don't be afraid to ask tough questions and to receive tough answers.

This brings us to a point we touched on earlier in the chapter. When you interview for jobs, you should be looking at employers as closely as they're looking at you. And if you don't like an employer, or you feel you're getting sucked into a demeaning interview game, you're entitled to politely end the interview and walk out of the interviewer's office.

"Did You Just Ask Me Why Buffalo Can't Sing?"

Infrequently, you'll encounter interviewers who want to know what you'd do in a bizarre hypothetical situation. You will realize that interviewers are playing interview games when they ask you strange, puzzle-like questions.

They may want to know what you think of the ancient feudal system and what kind of role it played in the evolution of agriculture in Europe and Asia. Or how you'd revamp the census system on a $500 budget. Or what you'd do if you were stranded in a snowstorm with a talking parakeet and a large ball of twine.

You will probably feel like asking them why they don't have enough to do with their time and where they hope to use the vast body of knowledge they must accumulate after ten or fifteen interviews based upon these questions.

In some ways, these interviewers may wish to inject creativity or individuality into their interviews. Or they may wish to see how much creativity or individuality you have. Don't let these questions throw you, and don't feel compelled to jump through hoops or demonstrate your intellectual prowess simply to find a job.

If you don't mind unusual interviews, or if you find them amusing, you may have found a quirky company that perfectly complements your personality and life-style. If you aren't attracted by this kind of thing, don't berate yourself for failing to answer these questions as the interviewer seems to wish you had.

Remember that you're an intelligent, motivated person who is simply looking for a job. You're not required to be some kind of entertainer who can discuss arcane topics at will. If you encounter an unusual interview in which the interviewer delights in asking you peculiar questions, don't despair. It may be that you've now pinpointed a company at which you don't want to work.

Luckily, it is rare, but you may encounter an interviewer who denigrates you and your accomplishments. This is less likely to happen at major corporations, but it can happen once in a while in any job search.

When I was looking for my first, and later my second, job out of college, I interviewed with a tremendous number of companies, thanks to networking, the classifieds and job banks. I had some great interviews which recharged me. I had some educational interviews which steered me in another direction. I had some exciting interviews through which I obtained job offers. And I had two interviews which qualified for the Interview Hall of Infamy because the interviewers were so harsh.

Luckily, the second time I encountered an interviewer who approached the interview, or maybe just me, with overt hostility, I was able to nip the interview in the bud. In that situation, I was interviewing at a large engineering firm for a job in the public relations department. Unfortunately, I interviewed with a sour, embittered man. He embarked on a tirade about how worthless public relations was, asked me skeptically if my previous employers (from a very large firm in a very large city) had attended college, and then proceeded to criticize my university for every flaw possible.

I sat there speechless and astonished, wondering why, if I were such a despicable sample of humanity, he would call me in for an interview. I also wondered why anyone would be dumb enough to take the job, and how I could get out of there. Finally, I interrupted, saying, "Mr. Jones, I really appreciate your taking the time to interview me," and walked out of his office. (I toyed with the idea of harassing the man for the rest of his life, but I decided I was too busy.)

Anyway, as rare as it is, you may encounter interviewers who do their best to snub you and to make you feel like you don't deserve any job, let alone the one available. There are two things to do here. The first is to keep your cool and the second is to keep your confidence.

You should never be rude to any potential employer because you never know when it will come back to haunt you. No matter what an interviewer might say to you, respond politely, even if it involves getting up and leaving. That is probably the best thing you can do when it is clear that the interview is not going anywhere.

You should also write these experiences off as strange job hunting occurrences. Don't begin thinking that there is something wrong with you, your resume or your job hunting methods. As with anything else, when you look for a job, you may encounter a few bad situations, and you can't let this ruin your job hunt.

After The Interview

How you follow up with employers after the interview is as important as how you followed up before you obtained the interview. It was by following up on your cover letters that you won the interview. Now, by following up on your interviews, you can win the job you've always wanted.

Thank you notes and phone calls are the two primary ways to maintain contact with an employer after an interview. Employers and career counselors agree that thank you notes provide a nice touch and help differentiate a job hunter.

"When I get a thank you note, I can tell that the individual has some class," comments Washington.

Thank you notes are vitally important, and they don't take much time. In your thank you note, you can be brief and to the point. You might start your note by telling the interviewer you enjoyed meeting him. Thank him for taking the time to discuss whatever it was he discussed with you, whether it was sales or financial management, and then put in a sentence or two about something you learned about the company.

For example, you might say, "I appreciate your telling me more about your marketing efforts and the methods you used to increase your customer base." Or, "I was interested to learn how you manufacture the stands for artificial Christmas trees, and I enjoyed touring your plant."

Adding a personalized sentence emphasizes that you took the time to write an individualized thank you note. It may also distinguish you from other job applicants if the interviewer talked to you about the company's marketing plans on a more in-depth level than with other candidates. Or gave only you a tour of the plant.

You can include a subtle "final sell" in your thank you note if it is exactly that—subtle. You might mention one of your three strong points and tie it in with something the interviewer mentioned. Or reiterate your interest in working there and pinpoint a specific area of the job that you found particularly appealing.

Thank you notes should follow the normal business letter format, and they should be typed on a standard eight and a half by eleven inch piece of paper. Handwritten notes, if written neatly on business-like stationary, are acceptable, but typed notes are the norm.

The second way to follow up after an interview is to call. Employers like job hunting candidates who are well-organized and assertive. They like job hunting candidates who approach job hunting as something that they can take charge of rather than something they passively react to. It is therefore to your advantage to check back in with an employer after an interview. However, you should get the interviewer's approval before you call.

At the end of your interview, when you are shaking hands with the interviewer, ask if you can call in two or three weeks to see if you're still being considered. If the answer is no, you clearly should not follow up. However, if the answer is yes, and many times it will be, you should call in the amount of time specified. If no time-frame is given, check back in with the employer in a week.

Call once or twice, and if you get through, say you'd like to see if you're still being considered. If you are, you can reiterate your interest in the job and briefly express your strong interest in working for the company. You can then wait for the company to contact you with a final answer. You've communicated your interest in the job, and you've brought your name to the employer's attention one more time. If you're not still being considered, thank the interviewer and say that you hope you'll encounter him or her again.

If the interviewer doesn't return your call after you've called two or three times, don't lose hope. It could simply be that the employer is busy. Call the employer back periodically, but be sure to carry on with the other parts of your job search.

Interviews are a vital, exciting, exhilarating part of job hunting. If you walk into an interview armed with self-confidence and with a knowledge of how to proceed, you can walk out with a job offer. The guidelines below will help get you started with your interview preparation so you can make every interview a success.

INTERVIEWING WITH CONFIDENCE

1. In the next few days, start preparing for interviews. If you have interviews scheduled, decide if you're going to research individual companies. If you're interviewing with a large corporation, or if you have time on your hands, go to the library and spend an hour finding out more about potential employers.

2. If you don't yet have any interviews scheduled, you can still prepare for any interview that might come your way. Identify your three strong points. Look over your resume and think back to your classes. Try to find at least five specific examples which demonstrate your strengths and achievements. Use examples from all parts of your life so that you can talk about successes in the academic world and in your summer jobs.

3. Develop an answer to each of the questions in this chapter. Start by answering them as you would answer if one of your friends had asked you. Next, polish your answer until it is positive, well-organized and coherent. If it fits, be sure to mention at least one of your strengths in each response.

4. Practice aloud with a friend. Ask him what he thinks of your answers.

5. Make sure you have all of the necessary interview clothes. You should also have extra copies of your resume in case the interviewer needs one. This is a good time to verify the addresses of all the companies with which you have interviews scheduled. Make sure you know where the company is located, and how long it will take you to get there.

6. You're ready to begin interviewing with confidence and poise! For information on how to make a decision after you receive several offers, read the next chapter.

CHOOSING A JOB YOU WILL LOVE...
I Thought I'd Just Withdraw Passing If I Didn't Like It.

"Choose a job you love and you will never have to work a day in your life."
—Confucius

Being happy in your job means choosing the job that is best for you. At times, this may seem easy. At other times, it may seem difficult and confusing.

In this chapter, we'll look at how to decide if a job is right for you. We'll also discuss how to field simultaneous job offers and what to say to potential employers. By looking both at how to make decisions and how to interact with potential employers, you can feel confident of your ability to choose a job you will love.

Making A Wise Decision

There are several ways you can make sure you're making a good decision about a job offer. First, you can look at each job you're offered and analyze its strong points and its weak points. Second, you can see how the job matches up with your mental list of things you want in a job. Third, you can listen to your emotional reactions, or your "gut feelings" about the job. Of course, if the last time you listened to your gut feelings you ended up swimming in a snake-infested lake in the middle of the night at an off-campus party, you may want to be a little careful on this one.

The best way to start making decisions regarding job offers is to analyze the strong and weak points of each job you're offered. Each will have a few things you will really enjoy and a few things you will not enjoy. This may sound like your calculus class, except, of course, there wasn't anything in that class that you really enjoyed.

"Make a list of everything you like and everything you don't like in the job you're considering, and write it all down," says psychologist Dr. Diane Goebes. "Assign a number to each trait and compare different jobs this way."

Developing Your Rating System

To be honest, using some kind of standard system to rate jobs for which I interviewed never occurred to me. I simply went to interviews, tried to decide whether or not the job looked good and then floundered my way through the decision-making process. The problem with this was that it was easy to get confused and to give one small aspect of the job an overblown importance.

You may find yourself doing this too. For example, you

might interview for a job in sales with a major corporation. During your interview, it might become clear that the job has five basic components. The job might involve interacting with the research department, learning about the company's products, developing a new client list, calling upon clients and making monthly presentations to your department. The first four parts of the job may appeal to you, but making a monthly presentation may not.

However, you shouldn't make the entire decision based upon the monthly presentation because this is only one-fifth of the job. In a situation like this, if you're able to use some kind of standard rating system for judging the job, you might see that it is heavier on the plus side than on the minus side. Of course, living at the beach and forgetting about the job search is heaviest on the plus side, but unfortunately, that is not an option.

There is an exception to this rule of judging the job on the sum of its parts and not on any one part alone. This is when one small part of the job looks so horrible that it would ruin any pleasure you could take in the rest of the job. Or when one small part of the job makes you feel so excited and fulfilled that it would nullify any qualms you would have about the rest of the job.

Situations like that are not too likely, so you should try to take a more balanced approach and come to a decision by looking at the complete picture.

In the job we've been discussing, if the thought of making an oral presentation makes you cringe, it's probably not a good job for you. However, if getting up in front of your boss and co-workers once a month simply doesn't appeal to you, but it's something you could deal with, this might actually be a good job for you. You may even be able to have your employer send you to a public speaking seminar to improve your skills after you land the job.

In developing a system for rating each part of a prospective job, you don't need to do anything complicated. Depending upon how you like to approach things, you might not even need to write anything down. As long as you have a firm idea in your own mind as to the factors you will use in judging your job options, you can develop a system that will work for you.

"Develop a list of criteria by which you will judge a job," advises career counselor Marilyn Goldman of Horizons Unlimited.

As you're faced with making decisions on job offers, you may be surprised what you will learn about your career goals. For example, you may find that you don't care what you're doing as long as you enjoy the people you work with. Or, you don't care about the people you work with as long as you're doing something that will affect the world. If you don't care about either what you're doing or who you work with, you might be able to replace one of your old professors.

If you find your career goals have changed slightly as you've progressed through your job hunt, you shouldn't feel distressed or confused. This simply means you've learned more about yourself from all of the work you've put into your job hunt.

For example, maybe you realized during an informational interview that you don't really want to work for a major corporation. Or that you've got to have a job which has a lot of variety or you'll be bored after two weeks. Take whatever it is that you've learned from your job hunt and incorporate it into your system for making decisions.

"I Want To Work In A Green Office In A Large Building By The Sea"

To come up with a standard method for judging each job alternative, make a list of things that are important to you in a job. You can then use this list to judge each job you're considering. Your list might include categories such as the personality of your future boss, the workload, the overall office atmosphere, the salary and the possibility for advancement. It probably shouldn't include the degree to which you can date your co-workers or your proximity to all the great after-work hangouts.

The key to making your rating system work is to tailor your list of important job qualities to your individual needs. Perhaps you're ambitious and you tolerate criticism well. You might rank the possibility for advancement as most important and the personality of your future boss least.

On the other hand, you may be a laid back person who is looking for a relaxed office atmosphere where you can achieve things in your own way. In this case, you might rank the personality of your boss as most important and the possibility for advancement least.

It's easy to toss around these job characteristics and talk about picking out which are the most important to you, but it can be hard to say since you haven't had a "real" job yet. However, you can figure out what matters to you if you'll think about the things you liked and disliked in your summer jobs.

I worked in an ad agency one summer, and I sat near a woman whose job required her literally to spend the entire day on the phone. I learned from that job that while I like to interact with other people, I probably would have developed a personality disorder, as well as some kind of crippling neck condition, if I ever had a job that involved that much phone work.

I remembered this after I graduated (yes, I know what an achievement that was) and it helped me steer clear of an entire range of jobs within the general field in which I was looking.

Try to remember what really bugged you in your summer jobs, and think about what really pleased you. Use these past experiences to figure out what you'd like in a job on a daily basis. I should probably break it to you now that it may be hard to find a job with adequate nap time.

Rating Your Offers

After you've decided how important you find each job characteristic, further develop your rating system. Using a set of numbers from one to five, with one being a positive reaction and five being a negative reaction, rate the job for which you've just interviewed.

Perhaps you would give the workload of a particular job a one, noting that there were a lot of exciting projects going on, but that no one seemed to work later than 6:00 p.m.

You might give your potential boss a two, noting that she is friendly and easygoing, but a stickler for small details. You might also give the office atmosphere a two, noting that it is a small office where people socialize outside of work and therefore must like each other.

You might give the salary a four, noting that it is lower than the other two jobs for which you've interviewed. Finally, you might give the possibilities for advancement a four, noting that no one in the office appears to have started out in the job for which you're interviewing.

When you jot down a number next to each job characteristic, include one or two explanatory phrases so you will remember why you assigned a job trait a particular number. At this point, it may seem like you'll remember everything from each interview. However, if you've had fifteen interviews in two months and you're trying to decide between three definite offers and one probable offer, you may have a hard time remembering the details of each job. You may also have a hard time remembering why you ever wanted a job in the first place.

Here's what your rating table might look like in this example:

A. Workload: 1 (I'd be doing 2 research projects at a time during busy season/people leave by 6:00)

B. Potential Boss: 2 (friendly, picky about little details such as format for interoffice memos)

C. Office Atmosphere: 2 (looks like they get along well)

D. Salary: 4 (lower than other 3 interviews I've had)

E. Potential for Advancement: 4 (small office—looks like someone else would have to leave for me to move up)

As you look over your ratings for the job in our example, you might decide the job isn't perfect, but it's a good one for you. You gave high ratings to the parts of the job that mattered the most to you and lower ratings to the parts of the job that didn't matter as much to you.

If this were the only job offer you had received, and you felt comfortable with it, you would probably want to accept it. If you were comparing this job to one that rated a one or a two for every category you evaluated, you'd probably want to take the other job.

It's important to note that the decision-making process is very personal. This same job might be a poor choice for someone who cares most about the possibilities for advancement and the salary and least about the workload, the office atmosphere and the personality of their boss. We'll talk more about this later.

Discovering Your Dream Job

The second way to make a wise decision is to see how the job you're considering matches up to the things you need in a job in order to be happy. As you develop your system for rating each part of the job, you should also develop a parallel rating system. In this parallel system, you can compare the job on which you're deciding to an imaginary checklist in your mind.

If it's important that you work for a company where individuality is prized and you can wear jeans to work on Fridays, put that on your mental list. If you want a job where everything is clearly defined for you and you know exactly what your boss expects of you, put that on your list.

This process of matching the job offer to your mental picture of the ideal job might not seem that helpful, but it will make your decision-making process much easier. Maybe you want to work in a fast-paced, quickly changing setting. Or you don't want a job that requires a lot of meetings and group efforts. Look closely at each job for which you've interviewed and see how well it matches up with what you want in a job.

"I've Got This Funny Feeling"

The third way to rate a prospective job is to look at your emotional reaction to the job. Even if all of the "facts" you unearth about the job are favorable, there may be something that keeps you from wanting to work there.

For example, you might interview for a job in engineering with a small construction company. The person you'd be working for may appear to be fair and reasonable, the hours about what you'd expect and the office environment a good one. But there may be some unspoken thought on your part that makes you hesitate to accept the job.

Maybe you never thought you'd work for a small company and you know you wouldn't be satisfied with one. Maybe the job looks nice enough, but for some reason, terribly boring. Even though these thoughts may seem illogical, include them in your rating system. If you aren't honest with yourself in rating the jobs for which you interview, you won't be able to make a balanced decision based on the complete picture.

You can also use these gut level feelings to decide that a job is a good one for you, even though the "facts" are not in the job's favor. For example, you might interview for a job with an ad agency, and everything will look great, except they'd be giving you the toilet paper account.

Maybe you never envisioned yourself spending all of your waking hours thinking about toilet paper, and, for this reason, you decide you could never take the job. Except the person you'd be working for was really great...And you'd have your own assistant...And there would be a chance for a promotion within six months.

After you weigh all of the aspects of the job, you might feel that other parts of the job compensate for its subject matter. Even though your emotional side is telling you to turn the job down, your rational side is telling you to accept. It's fine to go on gut feelings if you've looked very carefully at a specific job. In fact, it's important to listen closely to your gut feelings, especially when they're negative.

"Job hunters should listen to their gut feelings," says Dr. Goebes. "They have a right to reject the people, the location, the salary, the benefits or whatever."

Making Your Own Decision

As you use your rating systems, it's crucial that you accept or reject job offers to please yourself, not to please other people.

It can't be said too many times that you need to base your job hunting decisions on what you want since you are the person who will have to live with the consequences of your decision.

Finding out what it is that you want requires you to be candid with yourself. If you proceed honestly during the decision-making process and admit to yourself that large companies intimidate you or frequent travel tires you, you can weed out jobs falling into those categories and select a company at which you'd be happy.

However, if you're secretly afraid to weed out large companies, or jobs which require travel, because you think good job hunters shouldn't weed anything out, you may find yourself in a job for which you're ill-suited.

"Look at the pros and cons of each offer you're made," says career counselor Sherrie Pavol Bereda of Career Concepts. "Think about where you want to be five years from now."

As part of being honest with yourself, you also need to make sure you aren't accepting a job for the wrong reasons. There are a variety of "wrong" reasons to select a job. In general, any time you take a job because you feel you should, and not because you feel you want to, you have probably accepted a job for the wrong reason.

"Go with what's really important to you," suggests Dr. Goebes, "not with what should be important to you."

When you are trying to decide on a job, it helps to think of the job as something concrete which you could pick up and put on a huge scale. You can weigh the good parts of the job and the bad parts of the job. If most of the job appears to be bad, but there is one overriding factor which tips the balance of the scale so it is suddenly much heavier on the good side, this may be an acceptable job for you. Just use caution.

There are several overriding factors which have this effect

on job hunters, such as money or prestige. Its O.K. to accept a job on the basis of pay or prestige alone. However, you need to make sure that you aren't being temporarily blinded to the negatives of the job. If the charm of a high salary or a fancy title wears off, you may be left with a job so weighted down on the bad side that you can't believe you ever accepted it.

In other words, make sure that money, prestige or other factors don't become bad decisions for you. If you truly feel they alone would outweigh any negatives for you, then you're probably being honest with yourself and the decision is a good one.

If, on the other hand, you think the job looks miserable, but you feel you shouldn't turn down a high salary, you're probably about to make a bad decision. It all comes down to understanding your own needs and selecting a job that closely matches up with what you really want.

In some ways, it's hard to talk about good decisions and bad decisions, because, as we've discussed, every person's good decision is different. For an aggressive risk-taker who thrives on constant change and interaction with other people, a job in sales or state politics might be a good decision. A job in accounting or in research might be a bad decision. For someone who likes to work independently, the reverse would be true. And for someone who wants a job more in line with their collegiate life-style, a job as a professional party attendee or as a sleep research participant might be most appropriate.

There are a few ways to figure out what would constitute a good decision for you. If you're making a good decision, you're looking at every single aspect of the job. You're noticing the bad and the good, and you're making a judgment as to how the two would balance each other out.

As you make a good decision, you're also comparing the

job that you've been offered to your mental checklist of things you need in a job. You're listening to your gut feelings about the job. And you're doing what will make you happy.

Now that you've thought about your own decision-making process, you need to figure out how to best communicate the decisions you make to potential employers.

"Yes, I'll Take It"

First, it helps to remember that there aren't any rigid rules on how to accept or reject a job. As long as you're polite and honest, any way you choose to accept or reject a job offer will be appropriate.

In other words, there's no hidden protocol you must follow. Unlike that time you and your friends crashed that black tie party which turned out to be for distinguished alumni, and you ended up with your pictures splashed across the campus newspaper, you don't have to have that uneasy feeling that something you're doing is not quite right.

If you already know your answer is yes, you don't have to ask for more time to make it look like you're taking the offer seriously. Simply tell the employer you're excited to have been made an offer and yes, you're very eager to work for his company.

If you already know your answer is no, you don't have to delay giving the answer to soften the blow. As you've probably found, employers have a pool of job applicants from which to draw, and while they may be disappointed to lose you, they won't suffer for too long. So don't feel guilty about declining an offer that's not right for you.

When you say no, you can simply tell the employer you appreciate having had the opportunity to interview there, but you don't feel the job is an appropriate one for you at this time.

If you find it easier, you can say you're waiting on another offer or you've had something promising come up. However, it's best to be as honest as you can, and a straight no will usually suffice.

Remember to follow up your verbal response with a thank you note, even if you know you don't want to work at this company. Again, you never know to whom you may be referred if you impress someone during your job search, and valuable professional contacts can grow from brief meetings and even from turning down a job with a certain employer.

Finally, if you're not sure what your answer is, you don't have to make a decision on the spot. Instead, you can ask for more time so that you can make a good decision.

"Ask for a week to decide," recommends Pavol Bereda. "Never accept a job as soon as it's offered unless you're absolutely sure."

According to employers and career counselors, it's not unreasonable for job hunters to want to think about a job offer before giving an answer. These experts differed, however, on the amount of time they considered acceptable for job hunters to request before giving employers a decision. Some felt a few days would be the longest amount of time acceptable for job seekers to request. Others felt it would be O.K. to ask for as much as three or four weeks.

GE's Peter Bowen says, "After I make an offer, I give someone a month to decide, and if they need more time, I'll give them an extension."

Ford's Darrell Washington explains that the length of time available to job hunters to make a decision often varies with the job. "It depends upon the function. In some areas, like finance or engineering, we don't have the luxury to allow a lot of extra time to a job hunter [for decision making.] In other areas, we're not in such a rush."

The best solution, according to career counselor Susan Schubert of Schubert & Associates, is to ask the interviewer how much time you may have to think about it. "Rather than picking a time frame out of thin air, ask the employer how much time you have to make a decision."

When It Rains It Pours

This brings us to the second thing you need to remember as you communicate with potential employers. At some point, it is almost inevitable that you will receive a job offer from one employer while you're still waiting to hear from another employer.

This probably doesn't sound like much of a problem now, but figuring out how to deal with simultaneous offers ahead of time can save you anxiety and uncertainty a few weeks down the road. At that point, the timing of your response may be critical.

When you're trying to juggle simultaneous offers, you need to interact honestly with all of the employers involved. For example, if you get an offer from one company, and you're still waiting to hear from a second company, ask the first company for a little time to make a decision. You don't have to tell them you're waiting to hear on something else.

"It doesn't bother me if someone needs more time," says Bowen. "It's all part of the dialogue between myself and the candidate."

After buying some time with the first company, you can then call the second company and explain that you've received another offer, but that you wanted to wait until you had heard about their job. Politely ask for an update on your status.

"It's good when job hunters call back and let us know they've received an offer elsewhere," says Perpetual Bank's

Terri Goslin-Jones. "That gives us an opportunity to give them a decision in time."

Chrysler's John Stone agrees. "If someone gets an offer from another company before we've made a decision, they should call us and say they're being seriously considered elsewhere."

Luckily, most companies are fairly understanding when it comes to simultaneous job offers. Employers realize that you're interviewing with other companies too, and they know you will be getting other job offers and making some tough decisions.

"Honesty is the best policy," says Bowen. "I wouldn't want to lose someone, and if they needed to know if they had an offer, I'd do my best to accommodate them."

Perhaps the worst thing you could do when faced with two or more offers would be to make rash or hasty decisions. Maybe you don't feel like you can ask the first company for any extra time. The interviewer may have already told you the company is in a huge rush.

Perhaps you don't feel like you can ask the second employer to give you a decision more quickly. Your interviewer may have commented in an off-handed way that she couldn't stand it when job hunters called and pestered her after the interview.

You have several options here. You can play it safe and go with the offer from the first company without knowing if you're going to get an offer from the second company. Or, you can take a risk, turn down the first offer and hope the second company comes through with a job. Finally, you can go to Tahiti and forget the whole thing.

If you go with the first company and decide against the second company before you get an offer there, make sure the job available at the first company would really make you happy. Use your various rating systems to assure that you wouldn't get the job and spend the rest of your life wishing you'd waited on the second company.

If you make the other decision, that of turning down the firm offer from the first company and hoping for an offer from the second company, make sure the job with the second company is worth this risk. You should also consider how you'd feel about continuing to look for a job.

It might not be any big deal to you if you feel confident you will soon have other offers. However, if jobs appear to be tight in your region or you think you've exhausted all of your possibilities, risking losing both the first and second companies might not be worth it.

It's good to remember that up until the time you accept a job offer, you are still judging the company and the job it has available. It might sound as if it's too late for this, but you can tell a tremendous amount about a company and about the person who would be your boss by the way he or she reacts to your request for more time. Or, in the case of a second company from which you're hoping to receive an offer, your request for a more rapid decision.

If an employer is rude to you or angry because you're either asking for more time or asking for a more rapid decision, it might tell you what it's like to work at this company. If this makes the employer angry, how is he or she going to feel when you make the inevitable mistake or two that all new employees make? Or when you're sick and you miss a big meeting?

If you feel that an employer is trying to pressure you into making a quick decision, take this into account when you make your final decision. Luckily, most employers don't operate this way.

"We don't want to pressure a candidate into making a decision that might not be right," says Stone. "We're interested in finding a match."

Finally, trust your instincts. You've come this far, and you've probably learned a lot about what you want and what you don't want in a job. Take each aspect of the job into consideration, and proceed confidently. If you take your time, you can choose a job you will love. For successful ways to beat the job hunting blues that invariably seem to plague even the most motivated job seekers, see the next chapter.

Choosing A Job You Will Love

1. Start thinking now about what is important to you in a job. Do you care more about the office atmosphere or about the substance of your work? What did you like most about your summer jobs? What did you not like? Spend some time jotting down your thoughts about work.

2. Start keeping notes on your interviews. Even though it seems like you couldn't forget the details, write down your impressions of the people with whom you interview. Describe the major responsibilities of each job for which you interview.

If you had a chance to observe others in the office when you interviewed, did they appear happy? Busy? Energetic? Friendly? Even before you get an offer, go ahead and rate each job for which you interview. This will put you one step ahead when you do start getting offers.

3. Write down any questions that occurred to you after you walked out of the interview. If you get called back in, or if you receive an offer, it's perfectly appropriate to ask these questions now.

For example, would you be expected to pursue some type of graduate degree after you've worked at the company for a few years? If you took the job, would you get a performance and salary review in six months to a year? Would you be working with other new employees or would you be the only person on your level?

4. Congratulate yourself on your progress! You've come a long way, and you're now an expert job hunter. You're sure to find the right job soon.

Chapter 8
Avoiding Burnout

PICKING YOURSELF UP WHEN JOB HUNTING GETS YOU DOWN...
Is There Still Time For Me To Enroll For Next Semester?

"The secret of achievement is not to let what you're going to do get to you before you get to it."
—Anonymous

If you're sick of looking for a job and you feel you'll be forever doomed to trudging around a strange city with a stack full of unwanted resumes, you're in the right chapter. Sooner or later, everyone gets discouraged, but if you can keep a few important thoughts in mind, you can get past your job hunting burnout and forge ahead with your search.

In this chapter, we'll look at some practical, concrete tips for avoiding burnout as outlined by the experts. And we'll draw up an overall job hunting game plan so you can document your successes and keep yourself organized.

Do Something Every Day

First, above all else, there is one major way to successfully fight off those horrible job hunting blues: accomplish at least one thing related to your job hunt every day of the work week.

"Don't leave any stone unturned," advises Terri Goslin-Jones of Perpetual Bank. "Take some kind of action every day."

For example, keep up with the classified ads. When you get tired of job hunting, that's probably the first thing you let slide. Unfortunately, that's probably the best and most readily available resource.

If the classifieds aren't yielding a lot of opportunities, however, make it your goal for the day or for the week to find another source of job openings. Talk to a librarian about new avenues you could pursue. Look in the phone book for professional associations which might have a job bank.

If you'll stay busy in your job hunt, you'll stay committed, interested and ready to work. If you sit around and don't do anything to help yourself find a job, you'll soon lose your enthusiasm and your motivation. You'll then be trapped in the vicious circle of becoming discouraged because you don't have a job and becoming incapable of looking because you feel so discouraged.

If you feel like you've done everything to find a job that you could possibly do, you're moving in the right direction. However, as much as you hate to hear this now, there is always something new that you could be doing in order to find a good job. And it could be that little extra step that helps you find the job of your dreams. All it takes is one letter which makes it to the right person or one meeting with an employer who is looking for someone like you.

If you're suffering from job hunting burnout, you might not be able to think of any way to move your job search one more step forward. Why not develop a new mailing list of potential employers to which you can send your resume? Or begin calling employers to whom you sent your resume three weeks ago?

If you take all of these steps and you still have extra time on your hands, consider volunteering to work a few hours a week in a company similar to those in which you're interested. All of this activity will keep you from feeling that your job search, as well as your life, isn't going anywhere. Use these ideas as a springboard for getting yourself out of your job hunting rut. Maybe these suggestions don't apply to your job search, but there must be some kind of specific activity that does.

The more actively you pursue your job hunt, the richer the final results will be. Simply from a statistical viewpoint, the greater the number of resumes you send out, the greater your possibilities for uncovering the perfect job. And by doing one new thing every single day, you can increase your chances of making a great networking contact...or learning more about a certain aspect of your career field...or thinking of a way to improve your resume.

"Yes, I'm Still Alive"

You also shouldn't underestimate the value of interacting with friends and potential employers when you start to feel discouraged. Meet a friend for lunch and ask him if he has heard of any new jobs, either at his company or elsewhere. If he's on good terms with his boss and he works in the field in which you'd like to work, ask if he'd give his boss a copy of your resume to circulate to colleagues.

"Don't get discouraged if at first you fail in your job search," says General Motors' James Sturtz. "Pursue your interests and make yourself known."

If you make an effort to keep in touch with people throughout your job hunt, you'll be a lot more aware of different opportunities that might come up. You'll also keep yourself interested in the job hunt and fired up for another round of interviews.

Recognize Your Achievements

Second, employers and psychologists recommend that you don't focus on the things that haven't gone your way. Instead, focus on what's gone right for you and what you've gained in a week or two weeks or a month.

"People focus on the negatives and the rejections, but they should keep a list and look at what they've done every day," says Goslin-Jones. "It can help them keep track of their progress."

Since you haven't found a job, you might feel like you haven't accomplished anything. However, if you've been looking diligently, you've probably accomplished a lot. You've developed your resume and you've written your cover letter. You've decided what kind of job you want, and you've talked to people in the field about what's available. Considering that you were still in school a few short months ago, you've done a lot to further your career goals.

"You Mean You Weren't Born Into Your Job?"

Third, remember that you're not alone. Every single person who has a job today was once in your shoes. Because job hunting is an on-going process which requires a lot of soul searching, everyone gets burned out and discouraged with their job hunt at one point or another.

"I think it helps when job hunters remember that it's something everyone goes through," comments Dr. Diane Goebes. "It's a rite of passage and it gets easier over time."

What will separate you from the other job hunters out there is your ability to bounce back and to throw yourself into your search with renewed energy.

"I've Been Looking For A Job For Roughly Three Years Now"

Finally, keep your perspective. This is only one part of your life, although it may seem like everything right now. And you've probably only been looking for a few weeks or a few months. In the long run, that's not that much time.

It can take a while to find the best opportunity for you, and you shouldn't feel like everyone else fell into their job quickly or easily. If you keep looking for a job, and you do it regularly and enthusiastically, you'll find the organization that's right for you.

"One general time frame to use in finding a job is six months," says Sturtz. "Everyone will have a unique circumstance, but we find that to be fairly typical."

Job hunting can be difficult, slow-moving and discouraging, but ultimately, it's one of the most exciting, challenging and rewarding ways to discover what it is that you want to do with the rest of your life.

So, good luck, and happy job hunting! For details on how to organize your job hunt and chart your success, use the checklist below.

Getting To Your Job Hunt Before It Gets To You

Developing Your Home Office For Job Hunting

• Explore all of your options for photocopying or printing your resume and cover letters. Purchase any office supplies you'll need. Buy a telephone answering machine if you don't have one.

Developing Your Resume

• Maintain an adequate supply of resumes for sending to employers with your cover letter and for taking to interviews.

• Keep up with all professors, former employers, family friends, etc. who said they would serve as references. Update each person on your job hunting status; tell them when they'll be receiving calls.

If you're not finished with your resume, list three things you'll do here to finish it (e.g. meet with a professional resume writer, make a list of your major collegiate accomplishments, obtain sample resumes from a typesetter or printer).

Developing Your Cover Letter

• Determine the status of each cover letter you've sent out. Is it pending? Has it been rejected? Did the recipient of your cover letter direct you to someone else, either within her company or at another company? If so, did you follow up with a thank you note?

Make a list of three things you'll do regarding your cover letter (e.g. develop a new cover letter to send to large accounting firms, call 20 potential employers to whom you've already sent your cover letter, organize your files so you'll know what you have yet to do).

Finding Potential Employers

• Stay one step ahead of your job hunt by sending out a new mass mailing every three to four weeks. Do the appropriate library research; call and confirm the addresses and company names of each mailing recipient.

Make a list of three things you'll do to find potential employers (e.g. go through the phone book for company names, call alumni from your school to ask for prospects, join a networking or even a social group in order to broaden your web of contacts).

Networking

• Contact and meet with at least one new person a week. Obtain the names of possible contacts from a friend, from another networking contact or from the follow-up calls you place after you send a mass mailing. Have one or two concrete objectives when you meet with your contacts, such as finding the name of another person or getting some feedback on your resume.

Make a list of three things you will do to obtain a potential employer's name (e.g. ask a former professor, talk to a friend, look in the phone book).

Interviewing

• Practice your interview skills with a friend. Go through the list of interview questions; add on any new questions you've heard in the course of your interviews. Make a list of three things you need to do for upcoming interviews or for interviews you've already had (e.g. researching a company if it is a large one, determining your follow-up, writing thank-you notes).

Choosing A Job

• Rate all of the jobs for which you've interviewed using a system which works best for you. Make a list of three things you will do to further your decision-making process (e.g. develop a system for rating each job, look over your notes from previous interviews, decide what will make you happy in a work situation).

Make a list of additional thoughts you may have on your job hunt (e.g. perceptions of employers, goals for next week, things you really want in a job, reminders to buy office supplies).

Index

Sarah Hart